Shattering

RELIGION'S
HOLLOW SHELL

Miguel A. Alfonso, Jr.

XULON PRESS

Xulon Press
2301 Lucien Way #415
Maitland, FL 32751
407.339.4217
www.xulonpress.com

Scripture quotations taken from the New American Standard Bible (NASB). Copyright © 1960, 1962, 1963, 1968, 1971, 1972, 1973, 1975, 1977, 1995 by The Lockman Foundation. Used by permission. All rights reserved; King James Version (KJV) – *public domain;* New King James Version (NKJV). Copyright © 1982 by Thomas Nelson, Inc. Used by permission. All rights reserved; Amplified Bible (AMP). Copyright © 1954, 1958, 1962, 1964, 1965, 1987 by The Lockman Foundation. Used by permission. All rights reserved; The Passion Translation (TPT). Copyright © 2017 by Passion & Fire Ministries, Inc. Used by permission. All rights reserved. thePassionTranslation.com

Printed in the United States of America.

ISBN-13: 9781545674352

TABLE OF CONTENTS

ACKNOWLEDGMENTS

God my Father, Jesus my Lord, and Holy Spirit, my guide and friend.

My beautiful wife, Gloria, whose heart loves so purely. Thank you for your practical input and advice on this journey. God has helped me so much through your words and examples.

My son, Elijah, you've taught me a love I had yet to know and given me the best experience, being your dad. Your vibrant life exudes a joy that has been a treasure during my most difficult times. Thank you, my little buddy.

Mom, Dad, and Annette, your unconditional love throughout the many stages of my life has been God's heart expressed through you, and a foundation I know I can always depend on. Thank you.

Kevin Becker, your hunger for the authentic love and power of God, our deep friendship throughout life's journey has blessed me beyond what words could ever express. Thank you.

Jeremy Haynes, you've been an amazing example of childlike surrender to the Lord that has been a constant, loving, provoking for my spirit. Thank you for your surrender to Him and loyal friendship with me.

Thanks to the many incredible ministries, leaders, churches, and resources mentioned throughout this book and others I wasn't able to mention. You have been such an encouragement and example of the New Covenant supernatural lifestyle I once believed was just for biblical times alone or for a future time. More importantly, you've modeled that intimacy with Jesus is the key to this life and the next.

INTRODUCTION

This book is an overflow of my adventures with God, as my heavenly Father, Jesus as my Lord, and the Holy Spirit as my personal guide and friend. If you have any desire whatsoever to experience more of the tangible presence, love, and character of God in your *practical life*, this book is for you. Or perhaps you wish you did feel more hunger for the above – this book is also for you.

Scripture records countless supernatural encounters that many men, women, and children had with a *present* God. This *present God* reality surpasses the greatest things God did in the Old Testament. Religion today isolates God to those limitations. Instead, these encounters and supernatural experiences throughout the Bible are invitations extended to every redeemed son and daughter of God today.

Have you ever wondered, "If that's true, then why isn't it more evident in my church or in my life?" Or perhaps like me, for many years, you may have felt confident in various theological reasonings and beliefs to explain this question away. But I want to invite you on an adventure that the Holy Spirit has taken me on. One which started with Him asking me some very simple questions that challenged my practical life and theological beliefs. One that has changed my life forever as a passionate follower and lover of Jesus.

The first half of this book (Part I) is targeted to and beneficial for anyone, no matter what type of religious exposure or background you've been exposed to. You'll be challenged as we examine aspects of the Gospel, displayed in the lifestyle of a New Testament believer vs. the modern-day Christian culture and lifestyle we've grown accustomed to. You'll be provoked to desire "more of God" as I share some personal, supernatural encounters, experiences, and revelations from my own adventures. But you'll also see just how clearly incredible His invitation for you is, through the Gospel. We'll cover very practical ways you can access His Kingdoms' realm in your everyday life.

The second half of this book (Part II) is targeted and most beneficial for anyone with a Seventh-day Adventist background, exposure, or influence (and/or Jewish or Seventh-day Baptist background). It should only be read *after* the first half, being that, apart from the aspects of the Gospel shared in Part I, it remains absent of power to transform the heart. But *in the context of Part I,* Part II is extremely power-packed with revelation. Although I do share some encounters and experiences in Part II, a lot of the study is more specific to the Adventist background I grew up with, and ministered in for years, prior to this adventure beginning.

I believe your heart will be warmed by God's presence and love in a life-changing way as His Spirit draws you closer to Himself. His voice will be clearer to understand, His presence more easily felt and recognized, and your heart more passionately in love with anything and everything pertaining to Him.

CHAPTER 1

THE GOD BEYOND RELIGION

H e sat on the city's sidewalk, his back and head pressed against the building's cold, cement wall. So confused, lost, and alone, the tears ran freely down both cheeks. The smell of a nearby dumpster mixed with the fumes from traffic were all too familiar to him. He thought to himself, "How did this become the place I now call home?"

Just six months ago, he had a beautiful wife. They'd been married five years and had a three year old son. His two-story home, full-time job had provided a comfortable lifestyle… but now he was left with nothing. Without warning, his blissful life had been shattered, impossible to restore. He'd do anything to go back in time. Anything for just one more opportunity to be with his family.

A passerby handed him a cup of hot chocolate and a New Testament Bible. The words, "Jesus loves you, man." lingered in the breeze, sweetening the previously rank air. Strangely, he hadn't heard about Jesus. Having never been to church or conversed with anyone about God before he was intrigued. But as he read page after page about this Jesus, the depths of his heart were warmed. A piercing ray of indescribable joy, hope, and peace began to flood his soul, unlike anything he'd ever experienced.

Could it be that this same Jesus was still alive? Could Jesus heal and deliver him from his disease? As he read the book of Acts, he was thrilled to discover Jesus had left His followers with someone equally powerful: *The Holy Spirit*. Upon finishing the book, he said to himself out loud, "I have to find some believers so that I can be healed and filled with this Holy Spirit." He walked down the street and, to his surprise, found a church that had just begun their service. He was ecstatic. His utter darkness and despair could finally see a light at the end of his gloomy tunnel.

1

He found a seat and listened to a well-polished church program. The worship was beautifully collaborated with corresponding lights and effects. The announcements were filled with all kinds of upcoming activities and events. The sermon delivered by their humorous, entertaining pastor seemed to capture the congregation's attention. But when closing prayer was finished, and everyone began to go on their own way, the man was perplexed and ran up to the pastor.

"When do you guys do the stuff?"

The pastor replied, "What do you mean?"

"What do I mean?" the man replied, "The healings, casting out of demons, signs, wonders, and miracles – all that supernatural stuff that's in this book." He raised his New Testament to enlighten the pastor.

The pastor grinned and, with a slight chuckle, he replied, "We have the Word of God now, there's no need for those things anymore. God gave us his Word and that's all we need." He patted him on the back and excused himself to talk to someone else.

In shock and deep disappointment, he shuffled out of the church as if all the life had been drained from him. He returned to that alley. "I guess it was too good to be true," he sadly concluded. He spent another six unbearable months in that alleyway, enduring even more despair and depression then before.

But one sunny afternoon, he had an encounter with a believer, one filled with the Holy Spirit. From the second they began speaking, he knew this believer was different. His eyes burned with a fiery love and compassion as if he genuinely knew the pain, hurt, and turmoil the man had experienced in isolation. He spoke with a confident authority and power and seemed to radiate of something or someone from another world. The more they talked, the more alive he started to feel.

He was asked if he wanted to receive Jesus and the Holy Spirit to come and live inside of him. Without hesitation, he tearfully said, "I would love that." As the believer put his hand on the man's head, he was immediately overwhelmed with the presence of God. The incredible weight of his constant pain instantly lifted from him, as he experienced complete deliverance and healing from his disease and addictions.

From that day forward, he couldn't stop sharing what Jesus had done for him. He saw firsthand the power of the Gospel, beyond words on a page, or a polished church program. He had been liberated by it himself and believed nothing short of its power.

One day God challenged me with the thought, "What do people encounter when they encounter you?" Of the two examples of the Christian guys in the story, I was definitely the "hot-chocolate New-Testament passerby," not the second guy – the believer – with demonstrative, supernatural power and love. In fact, I haven't believed the second guy was a reality for our day in age. Maybe in the Bible, but surely not today. At most, maybe I could believe that to be a rare, isolated exception in a foreign country. But should it be the *exception*? Or should it be the *rule* of a true biblical believer?

There is so much in the world that is said *about* God. If it's Christmas time or Easter, you can easily find a church putting on a nativity play or a resurrection program. Every week, millions of Christians gather at a church to worship. In spite of that vast quantity of churchgoers, how many of these people, how many of these churches, make the living God really and truly the *center* of their worship? Do they actually encounter His supernatural, liberating, miraculous presence there?

Please don't misunderstand, I do believe God will and has always used whatever and whomever He can to reach us, because of His persistent love for us. But has our current understanding of His ability to connect caused us to settle for far less than what He died to give us? What if the reasoning we've used to explain away the lack of God's supernatural power and presence in our lives originated from previous religious leaders? Those leaders may have also tried to make sense of their obvious lack, when compared to the book of Acts. What if the very fear of being one of the "deceived elect" in the last days, was the very thing we'd become, as evidenced by the clear contrast of what we call *church* today, versus what's powerfully modeled in scripture?

Leonard Ravenhill once said, "Many people go to church to talk about God instead of actually going to meet with God." Is it possible what most of us currently call *church* is simply a place where we recount what the God of Scripture once *did* and once *said,* rather than what He is *doing* and is *saying*? Is that the level of our expectancy we have when heading to church? Or do we truly believe, in our heart of hearts, we are going to meet and encounter the God of the universe in a *new* and *fresh* way?

In my walk with the Lord, I've spent most of my life believing I knew what it meant to be "born again," filled with the Holy Spirit, and to understand what a spiritual life was. But over time, I wondered, "Have I become a container of intellectual, theological, head knowledge *about* God, rather than the deeper spiritual-substance Scripture describes? Have I exchanged *true spirituality* for powerless religion? Was such an exchange the "norm" in my religious circle? We all had the same degree of expectancy for church – listen to announcements, sing a few songs (while struggling to actually pay attention to the depth of what we were singing) and then sit down to hear a message *about* God.

Does the Holy Spirit move in this kind of degree of expectancy? Yes, but only to the degree of our expectancy and nothing more. In our heart, we feared to permit the Holy Spirit to move beyond the predictable boundaries we considered *safe*. Without even realizing it, we'd had years and even decades of only seeing and experiencing the Holy Spirit to a small degree. Many of us have been shallow and, therefore, had no hunger or desire for more involvement with the Holy Spirit. I honestly didn't even know what *the more* of the Holy Spirit's presence would look like if He had shown up. My first reaction probably would have been, "That must be demonic."

But isn't that how religion has always responded to the supernatural? In reading any of the numerous accounts of Jesus – or one of His disciples – demonstrating a miracle, sign, or wonder of God's power, you'd discover the very first ones to cast doubt and label it as demonic were the most biblically-learned scribes and Pharisees. Jesus warned that this would always be the result of His power-demonstrating disciples. He said, "...if they persecuted me they'll persecute you..." (Jn 15:20).

In the church I was raised in, we were vehemently warned about the many deceptions the devil would muster up in the last days and how he would deceive even the "very elect." I repeatedly heard, and even preached, scriptures like, "*Even the devil can appear as an angel of light.*" As a denomination, we prided ourselves with our cherished church history from our pioneers who had forewarned us of the many deceptions to come from the majority of other "nominal Christians." That background left me scared for anything "more" or different as far as a relationship with the Lord, Jesus, or the Holy Spirit. What I knew as the "norm" was living in fear of the devil deceiving us like he'd "already done to the other churches," according to teachings. This was so ingrained that, despite quoting many of the *right scriptures*, my lifestyle and church culture itself painted a picture of a very powerful devil versus a very weak God, who wasn't operating in power like He once had.

We'd try to compensate for the obvious void of God's power by saying, "Well, when the latter rain comes *then* we'll have power again." We'd read and even recite scriptures that said, "and Jesus healed them all," and talk about how *one day* He'd be coming back for us and *in heaven* there would be no more death, sickness, or disease.

What we believed was the big, bad devil who has been the cause of sickness, disease, and death (Jn 10:10), will keep oppressing us until Jesus comes back, so "just hang on to this hope, brother and believe in *that day*."

Despite the popularity of such views in many similar churches today, one must deny the clear teachings of Scripture, with regard to the topic of the Holy Spirit's power and supernatural fruit, in order to embrace such beliefs as I had.

Yet, how could such human reasoning and unbelief be perpetuated decade after decade and remain so uniform amongst members of many churches worldwide? One way is by teaching and believing that questioning our unique position of beliefs equals giving in to the devil's deception, because as we were told, "All he is trying to do is get us to doubt *our truths*." But what if the real deception is actually in the "Don't question any of our beliefs" part? There are plenty of biblical and practical reasons to question *any* powerless teachings, no matter how credible any man, preacher, prophet, or organization claims them to be.

I've seen the most paralyzing mistake in most organized religion today – the silencing and ignoring of the large elephant in the room, which is that the authentic Gospel has *always* been *preached* and *demonstrated* by the presence and power of the living God. In fact, it's this very power of God that exposes dry, powerless religion, which has always attempted to counterfeit the active works of our *living* God.

In effort to defend powerless religion, so many of us have concluded, "Well, in the last days, the supernatural demonstrations of God will decrease and we will have only the Bible as credible proof." But where is that stated in the Bible? It's not. Later, we'll cover where that teaching actually came from and how church leaders used it to explain away our own lack of experiences with God's miraculous power. But scripture *never* says the tangible power/presence of God would one day expire or decrease in the last days – but instead that it would increase.

"Greater things than these you will do," Jesus said.

Joel said , "It will come about in the last days That I will pour out My Spirit on all mankind; And your sons and daughters will prophesy, Your old men will dream dreams, Your young men will see visions. Joel 2:28.

So many Christians are still waiting for this "last days" proclamation from Joel to come. But in Acts 2:15-16 on the day of Pentecost, (the day the Holy Spirit came down on all of the disciples as fire), Peter tells the people,

"[15] ...these men are not drunk, as you suppose, for it is *only* the third hour of the day;[16] but this is what was spoken of through the prophet Joel..." and then he quotes the Joel 2:28 passage. Note, this Joel passage regarding the "last days" has already come and has been here since the day of Pentecost.

Paul says, in Romans 15:19, "in the *power* of *signs* and *wonders*, in the *power* of the Spirit; so that from Jerusalem and round about as far as Illyricum I have fully preached the gospel of Christ."

To say, "Signs, wonders, and power of the Spirit will decrease in these last days because they were mainly for Jesus' time," is to say, "We're just not going to demonstrate the *full Gospel* Paul mentioned or that Jesus and His disciples modeled." Humanly, it's much easier for a religion to focus on the aspects of the Gospel that don't actually require the real tangible presence, power, and endorsement of God and, simultaneously, magnify the parts we can teach and preach on our own without Him. But Scripture does not support such a stance. In fact, this scripture states the exact opposite:

> "my message and my preaching were not in persuasive words of wisdom, but in *demonstration of the Spirit and of power*, [5] so that your faith would not rest on the wisdom of men, but on the *power of God*." 1Cor.2:4-5 NASB.

Notice, without "demonstration of the Spirit and of power," one's faith merely rests on the wisdom of men. If what we are being taught in our beliefs is different than the same biblical presence and power of God, then that is the very questioning we should have. The alternative is to stagnantly float on all the religious rationales we've clung to, distracted by our man-made religious activity, to give us just the right amount of religious security to keep us numb to the actual reality of our condition. That is exactly what I had subconsciously done for many years, not only as a church member, but as an active preacher and teacher in ministry.

Unknowingly, I had adopted a polished culture of unbelief in my life, which was the very reason "the signs, wonders, and power of God..." weren't following me as with Jesus' disciples. I believed in a God who was, and a God who will come, but not the God who *is*. Not a living, tangible, powerful Christ – and it showed in what I emphasized, not only in my ministry, but in my personal life. It showed in how I spent my time, resources, and priorities. But then, in the midst of my vulnerable awakening to spiritual bankruptcy, something began to happen that changed everything.

I started to experience His tangible presence and power personally, through healings, signs, wonders, dreams, visions, and supernatural encounters. Occurrences happened, things that I once could only refer to, in the Scriptures, as "that time God spoke directly and supernaturally to men." Now I realize how much He loves to be intimately involved in our day-to-day lives. He loves to speak to us in supernatural ways that remind us of how loving and powerful He truly is. I'm sharing many of my experiences in this book, not merely to tell you all He's done for me, for us, but so your ceiling of expectancy of what He gave you at Calvary will be raised to biblical truths and standards. Then, it will become more a part of your life too. I invite you to take a deep breath, clear your head for a moment, and pray this prayer from your heart:

Holy Spirit, I need you. You've promised to be my personal guide into ALL truth and I'm asking You for discernment, wisdom, and a fresh revelation of who You are. I want to encounter You in a deeper way than ever before, so that I'll never again be the same. Give me eyes to see, and ears to hear what Your voice, and Your Word is saying to me now, so that Your truth will set me free from any and every distraction that is keeping me from You. I pray in Jesus' name, Amen.

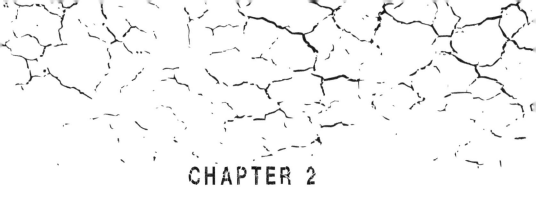

CHAPTER 2

HIS SUPERNATURAL POWER NOW

We've all seen news programs on T.V. exposing televangelists for fraudulent use of money, resources, and even healings. It's such a sad thing to see people abusing their claim to holiness to deceive people for financial gain. But I've also seen that, like a lot of media today, sometimes what they are choosing to highlight in their "breaking story" is their own twist to get more views and provocative headlines. Only a real seeker of truth will dig beyond the surface being presented to the public as *truth*. Perhaps you've flipped through the channels as I have, and paused on a broadcast where healings were taking place. As the evangelist laid his hand on someone's forehead, they'd fall over. You thought to yourself, "What a load of garbage." In my journey, I've found in some cases where that's truly all it is. But I've also been surprised at many such experiences I've found to truly be God's work.

If a small, pink pill like Benadryl, an anti-histamine, can cause a person to become overwhelmed by sleep as a side effect, how much more could the tangible presence and power of God affect our physical bodies? We have faith in so many *natural* things that affect our body, such as inhaling certain essential oils, taking medications, drinking alcohol, and so forth. Yet, with God, we limit His ability to affect our mind, soul, and body when He manifests His power.

Is it possible that the authentic, supernatural working of God is *sometimes* being labeled as garbage when it isn't? Wouldn't it be just like the devil to use the garbage to keep us distracted and in unbelief of the truly authentic? I have found that is exactly what he has done and continues to do. In fact, think of the numerous times in Scripture where the religious leaders and people of Jesus' day labeled His miraculous works as "from the devil."

In my walk with God these last few years, I've been completely blown away and humbled by the amount of supernatural things God is currently doing all over the world. What I've personally witnessed in the United States alone has completely changed my level of expectancy of God's ability to manifest His power and presence to the same biblical examples I had previously only read about in Scripture. I've found myself repeatedly saying, "Wow, God, I had no idea you were still this active." But then again, if the only news we are tuned into is everything except God's news, then of course I wouldn't know any different, nor would I be provoked to experience anything more for myself. I believe the devil wants to keep believers in disbelief of the supernatural and remaining out of touch with the reality of what the living Holy Spirit is currently doing. If that were to happen, the very power that crushes Satan and his works, would be immobilized in our lives. I believe many of us have become alienated to God's supernatural workings, for the above reasons and perhaps from experiences we've had – such as stepping out in faith to pray for someone's healing and afterwards felt like it didn't work. Then, like I did, we'd make up a theology to explain that experience away.

Regardless of your initial intent in reading this book, I challenge you to "try God" out. Only, this time, do it in a different, more practical, real, and vulnerable way. I challenge you to take *every* time you pause for an aloud prayer, as a serious moment between you and God. I challenge you to believe He's truly present with you and even at the edge of His seat, inviting you to live and walk more fully into all that He has created you to be, and all that He died for you to have. My desire for you is to build a greater faith in the one who is still that same miraculous, powerful and real living Christ that He was yesterday, is today, and will be forever.

I invite you now, to truly be open-minded and open-hearted, entrusting your doubts, worry, and anxieties to the one who has promised to be your personal guide into all truth: The Holy Spirit.

Pray out loud:

> *"Holy Spirit, please take the lead. Shed light in the areas of my thinking that have become darkened with unbelief. Soften in me what's hardened and jaded from past negative experiences and misperceptions of the supernatural, so that I may receive the truth of*

> *what You say on these things, and so that the truth*
> *will set me free from any and every lie of the enemy,*
> *in Jesus' name, Amen.*

Numerous scriptures reveal that the supernatural was never introduced as a once-in-a-while exception, but as the actual *lifestyle* of a new-covenant believing believer:

Mark 16:17:

> [17] These signs *will* accompany/follow those who *have believed*: in My name they will cast out demons, they will speak with new tongues; [18] they will pick up serpents, and if they drink any deadly *poison*, it will not hurt them; they will lay hands on the sick, and they will recover."

Jesus didn't say "these signs *may* follow those who have believed but rather WILL follow those who have believed. I'd been going to church week after week, preaching year after year, hosting Bible studies time and again, yet I couldn't help but notice there were *none* of these signs that Jesus promised showing in my life, nor the lives of fellow believers I went to church with.

So, either He was mistaken, or I needed to re-examine what I believed in, because it obviously wasn't the same "belief" Jesus was describing. The definition of insanity is doing the same thing over and over while expecting different results. Well, I guess I had become pretty religiously "insane" as I held tightly to all the doctrines, beliefs, and theories I had learned, despite their clear lack of the fundamental fruit of the Gospel of Jesus Christ.

Matthew 10:1,7-8:

> Jesus summoned His twelve disciples and gave them authority over unclean spirits, to cast them out, and to heal every kind of disease and every kind of sickness....[7] And as you go, preach, saying, 'The *kingdom of heaven is at hand*.' [8] Heal *the* sick, raise *the* dead, cleanse *the* lepers, cast out demons. Freely you received, freely give.

Notice the way "kingdom of heaven" is used isn't referring to the *physical place* of heaven, but instead the realities of heaven being manifested here through supernatural healings, deliverances, and other works of God. If you look up the word *kingdom* in the New Testament, you'll see many other examples of Jesus and the disciples using this word to encompass the supernatural realm where God's presence and power dwells. Yes, we also know there is a physical place called heaven, too, but in the New Testament, *kingdom* is often referring to the supernatural qualities and realities of that place overflowing here into our physical earth and even out from our very own lives.

Jesus was filled with the Holy Spirit and became an "access point" of heaven's *kingdom* realm as He walked the earth. In fact, in Luke 17:21, when the Pharisees ask Him about the kingdom, He plainly says, "it's in your midst," or as other versions translate, "it's already among you," or "it's within you." In essence, when we hear Jesus saying, "The kingdom of heaven is at hand," it's Him saying, "God's presence and realm is *now* here and within your reach."

But, know that this didn't stop when Jesus left. He came to establish His kingdom on earth, which He did by dying for our sins, so that His Spirit could continue to extend His kingdom's realm/realities through inhabiting our bodies as it did His. We see this displayed in the last Scripture (Mat. 10:7-8) and the first New Covenant/Christian church in the book of ACTS, who were filled with the *same* Holy Spirit and became extensions of the kingdom, just as Jesus was.

Prior to Jesus' death on the cross, humanity could only see glimpses of this and hope on promises of such an incredible reality. In fact, only the high priests could even come close to such an encounter but just once a year in the most holy place compartment of the Old Testament sanctuary. But since the cross, this reality is now here – within our reach. For us to continue to wait for it, as the Old Testament/Old Covenant believers had to, is to reject the present supernatural realities He died to give us.

Today, as our surrender to the Gospel is a fuller "Yes" to the presence and power of the Holy Spirit, we too, can become extensions of God's supernatural, healing, all-powerful realm of the kingdom. This is why the Church is referred to in Scripture as the *body of Christ*. The Holy Spirit is always looking for more "bodies" to fill and possess with heaven's supernatural qualities and power. This is one of the most incredible aspects the Gospel has accomplished for us to experience. It has always been about the supernatural presence of the *living* God, restored in us and through us.

As God continued to convict me of such clear instruction to go heal the sick, (and more,) I realized how immobile I was due to years of unbelief in my life and theology. These negative thinking patterns quenched these verses and truths, which had become nothing more than "something someone else once experienced."

I then sought for the *magical* wording in prayer to use for the healings and miracles to work. "Perhaps if I said, "in the name of Jesus" in a deeper tone, it'll work." But no, that was just the religious part of me seeking for another formula. But God began to show me His desire was to recalibrate my mind and beliefs to what His Word actually says on these matters, instead of what my religious culture and church had.

As I grew in His Word regarding this topic and more about our supernatural identity and authority as sons and daughters of God, I began to see miracles, healings, and people become radically free from pain, injury, and sin as I prayed for them. From my wife's back problem which had left her on the floor, unable to walk, to our friend's two-year old, who had to have continuous breathing treatments just to breathe through each night, to various strangers with injuries, sickness, etc., that I'd be led to pray for in the grocery store, workplace, and other public places. I was seeing the Gospel bring a tangible deliverance as Jesus had always demonstrated for us to do. I was seeing His kingdom realm truly "at hand" and extended through each encounter I witnessed before my very own eyes.

I realized the more in tune I could be with God's presence, the easier it was to allow the way He wanted to supernaturally love or extend the kingdom to a person in front of me. In fact, the more my focus was on His presence, the more supernatural fruit would spontaneously happen. (Chapter 5 will discuss more about practical time in His presence)

> In Genesis 3:8, after Adam and Eve sinned, it says, "⁸ They heard the sound of the LORD GOD WALKING IN THE GARDEN IN THE COOL OF THE DAY, AND THE MAN AND HIS WIFE *hid themselves from the presence of the LORD GOD* among the trees of the garden."

The devil's goal was in deceiving them into an alienation from the presence of God. At the root of sin, is separation from the one in who's image and likeness we were created (Genesis 1:26). Apart from His presence there is no life. Sure, by grace we are physically breathing and physically walking around, but *the quality of our life is contingent to the degree we are aware of and commune with the living presence of God.* Notice, God came to walk and talk with Adam as they always had. There was an actual tangible experience of His presence that would fulfill everything man had been created for. *Every human cell finds its highest satisfaction in the presence of God.* We are designed to be in union with God, to walk with Him and radiate His very image and likeness as a byproduct. But, apart from this intimate relationship, man had believed the devil's lie, and now was ashamed (Gen 3:10) of their bodies, which God had made to bear His glory, image, and presence.

Like Adam and Eve, many of us "believers" have believed the many lies of shame and condemnation about who we are, who God is, what He is currently doing or not. We've mustered up so many man-made methods to cover up our shame and lack of intimacy with the Lord, while operating day-to-day life *apart* from His presence. We claim the identity of a believer, thinking our mere intellectual, theological head-knowledge of certain doctrine and Scripture is what qualifies us. Jesus addressed the religious leaders regarding this very mistake saying,

> [39] you search the Scriptures because you think that in them you have eternal life; it is these that testify about Me; [40] and *you are unwilling to come to Me so that you may have life.*" (Jn 5:39-40)

These weren't just church members Jesus said this to. They were well-respected men of the highest religious endorsement of the day and known for their extreme study. They would have memorized of all the books of Moses by the age of fourteen. Yet, Jesus basically told them, "You've fallen in love with the *word of God*, but are far from the presence of the *God of the word.*"

Like I've seen with myself, many people, although sincere, have fallen into this same exact trap, and as a result, lack the supernatural fruit described in previous texts, the "signs that follow them that believe." We've come up with many *man-made endorsements* that *we* consider to be spiritual, while having an obvious lack of God's presence and power. We've conceived and created many denominational names (over 500) to try and distinguish our beliefs over another's. But no matter how popular or how esteemed that may be in our current circles of friends and family, *heaven is either truly endorsing it or it is not*. Our analysis can be simple, viewing it the way God's Word has told us: "These signs will follow them who have believed..."

> *If what we believe is in line with what Jesus was referring to, His presence and supernatural power will surely endorse and empower our lives, families, ministry, and churches.*

Jesus says in John 16:12-13, [12] "I have *many more* things to say to you, but you cannot bear *them* now. [13] But when He, the Spirit of truth, comes, *He will guide you into all the truth*; for He will not speak on His own initiative, but whatever He hears, He will speak; and *He will* disclose to you what is to come."

Jesus could have written a completely flawless set of New Testament Scriptures and said, "Here, read, study, and apply this and you guys should be good to go." But instead, He said that the "many more things" He had to tell us, would come through a *personal* guide, comforter, friend. The Holy Spirit. Notice He didn't say to the disciples, "and He (Holy Spirit) will guide you to write scriptures, which will then guide you to all truth," but instead, "The Holy Spirit Himself will be our guide because He will not speak on His own initiative but whatever He hears, He will speak and will disclose to you what is to come."

Notice how Jesus depicts relationship with Holy Spirit: a relationship in which we are *constantly hearing what He is saying to us*, because what He desires is a *present relationship experience* that allows Him to share what He is hearing Jesus say to Him. Nobody knows Jesus as intimately as the Holy Spirit, therefore, if we desire to follow, obey, and love Jesus there is *no other way* then to receive the present-day experiences and realities the Holy Spirit longs to bring us into. (Any previous methods in the Old Testament/Old Covenant all pointed forward to this present day reality of the Holy Spirit.)

What Jesus did for humanity by dying on the cross over 2,000 years ago is incredible. But the Holy Spirit is the present-day tangible presence of God that brings those Gospel realities and truths into a *personal, real, supernatural, powerful, experience* for us today. All of the spiritual blessings we read about in Scripture... the access to so many supernatural things, and the *direct* communication between God and man which has now been restored, is only made a *living reality* by intimate relationship with the Holy Spirit. This is why the Holy Spirit is the main theme emphasized throughout the New Testament and New Covenant. It is so important we learn His ways and His voice or we are missing out on the full experience as a believer of Jesus – and Jesus deserves His full reward. The Holy Spirit is the key taking us from powerless religion to the living realities, which were promised for hundreds of years and that Jesus died to give us.

You will hear me use the term *intimacy* a lot throughout this book. Humanly, we may only think of this word as the physical act between a man and woman. Though that physical act is the closest kind of physical expression between a man and woman, in marriage there is an intimate knowing of each other that is unlike any other relationship on earth. That intimate knowing is a special love and depth of conversation and intuition connecting one another as a result of many trials, victories, growth, time, and experiences shared just between two people. No other earthly relationship between siblings, parents, or friends is like this. Scripture calls the church *The Bride of Christ* for this very reason. Jesus wants to have such a present-tense, intimate, special connection with Him, unique to each of us. Such a purity reflects just how close our life is to His.

> *I've found at the root of powerless religion is a lack of experiencing and knowing God's present presence and present voice.*

The people who opposed the person of Jesus Christ and His anointing of the Spirit were those who had *once heard* from God but were no longer *hearing* from God. In other words, they monumentalized the last time the saw God move or heard God speak (through

Abraham, Moses, prophets, and others) and clung to these events as their own identity and standing with God, while remaining completely out of touch and apart from what God was *currently* doing and saying, through His very own Son, Jesus. They heard those stories and made it the ceiling of their own reality, rather than a foundation to develop their own experience with the living God.

This is clearly shown at the beginning of Jesus' ministry. In Luke 4:14-30, Jesus came out of His wilderness experience victorious and "in the power of the Spirit," (vs.14). He went to the synagogue (church) He'd grown up in, to read the Scripture reading of the day "as was His custom," (vs.16) But the difference, was He was full of the power of the Spirit. When He finished reading and sat down, "every eye of everyone in the synagogue was on Him," (vs. 20) They were in obvious awe and wonder of this supernatural empowering of the Holy Spirit demonstrated by Jesus who they'd seen grown up and read that same Scripture before. Jesus tried to explain that particular Scripture they were always reciting was "now fulfilled" in that supernatural encounter with Him. But that didn't go over so well, and in fact, after mocking Him, they tried to throw Him off a cliff.

They had no problem with Jesus of Nazareth, who was Joseph's son. But they wanted to kill Jesus Christ. *Christ* means, *anointed* or, literally in the Greek, "smeared with God/God's presence." He read the exact same scripture as always, but instead He was actually anointed/smeared with God's presence as Verse 14 pointed out, "in the *power* of the Spirit."

It's much easier to keep a particular lifestyle, habits, T.V. shows, and movies when we just meet each week to recite what God *once said and did*. But, when confronted with what God *is* saying and what He *is* doing, one is faced with a decision. In the Scripture reference above, the scholars decided, "We'd rather keep our manmade dignified belief and spiritual assessment of ourselves than realize the need for an actual experience with the present presence and voice of God."

Here was a church filled with respected religious leaders, veteran believers who could proudly recite their church's history like nobody's business, yet they displayed nothing more than the anti-Christ (anti-anointing) spirit. That's why the spirit of religiosity is so deceiving. It knows all the "right scriptures to quote," which of the Bible promises to recite and when to say them, what religious clichés and phrases to say to fit the current religious molds of the day. The religious spirit knows what politically-correct Christian phrases to offer.

Everything can function as smooth as silk (in the eyes of man, at least) in the church settings where this religious spirit is alive – UNTIL, anyone anointed, smeared with the presence of God, with signs and wonders following their life, shows up at church. Unfortunately, the response the majority of the time will probably be exactly how they treated Jesus. "Get Him out." There's just too much religious pride to swallow. Too many years, time, and theological webs to challenge. Too many fears of being labeled as so many others who'd challenged the religious system that are now modern heretics to the denomination.

I submit to you the previously stated question: Are you experiencing God's tangible presence each day? Can you actually hear His *living* voice? Are the *basic* signs and wonders of the Gospel following you? Can one who is sick, diseased, or demonized, encounter the same *living Christ* they read about in these passages, at your church? In your path? I know my answer was a painfully, humbling *no*.

> *Although I could point them to Scripture, I couldn't introduce them to the living one behind those Scriptures because I myself wasn't experiencing Him that way.*

Please understand I'm not saying by any means that I have "attained" to the fullness of this reality, but I can say I've never seen and experienced as many breakthroughs, healings, signs, wonders, supernatural encounters, dreams, visions, and angelic activity as I have now... and they increase more and more every day. (I'll be sharing many of these experiences throughout this book.) I'd started to realize that it is imperative and absolutely vital for me to be hearing God's present voice and to be experiencing His present presence 24/7 if I was going to align myself with the New Covenant believers of Scripture.

The religious leaders missed and even denied the supernatural power of God – which was evident all around them and right in front of them. Is it possible so many people in God's churches today also overlook, or are oblivious to, His supernatural power and presence?

Religious leaders believed it happened in the past with Moses, Abraham, and others. They realize that one day in the *future* it will happen again, but they continue to deny His power in the *present*. Is the Holy Spirit grieved by our unbelief in His present day abilities? I didn't realize I had so many religious theologies and hurdles quenching the present power and presence of the Holy Spirit in my life. But as He revealed them to me, I began to see firsthand just how His power truly is manifested in the present.

I believe God wants to touch you in a way you've never experienced. I believe He wants to take you beyond your intellect and into many tangible encounters with His presence and voice. Will you posture your heart for a moment to be more vulnerable to the Holy Spirit's presence? Invite Him to make Himself more real to you as you pray this out loud:

Holy Spirit, I welcome Your tangible presence into my life. I'm sorry if I've put my trust in anything or anyone, other than You, to guide and lead me in my walk with God and in my understanding of scripture. I'm sorry if I have even mistakenly dishonored Your fruit by calling them demonic or by hardening my heart to them in fear of being deceived. Help me to have more faith in Your capability to lead my life than in the devil's capabilities to deceive me. I want to invite you to have Your way. Soften my heart, incline my ears to hear You more clearly. Stir me up to receive Your presence to a greater depth, and to have an increased sensitivity to You being here in the present, with me right now, in Jesus' name, Amen.

CHAPTER 3

HIS PRESENCE IS SURELY ENOUGH

In 2004, I entered into ministry. Although I had been in church my whole life, I had just begun to experience the transforming power of the Gospel for the first time. I was passionate to share the Gospel with the world. Just before entering ministry, I experienced God's hand of grace delivering me from my rebellious streak of partying, weed smoking, and drinking. Prior to this, I had tried all the popular religious methods of "sanctification," only to fail and be discouraged time and time again. But now I had experienced the supernatural heart transplant as described in Ezekiel 36:25-27, and was set out to declare the good news and how God is able to change us from the inside out, rather than the outside in. So many times, even now, God reminds me of the simplicity of this truth. The reality is, this was just the beginning of me experiencing the real Gospel of Jesus Christ vs. powerless religion and ritualistic traditions.

I became more "theologically trained" through Bible college, in depth study, and working in various churches for various conferences. I enjoyed sharing what I understood about the Gospel. I loved giving Bible studies, writing Bible studies, and at other times, writing in-depth theological articles or rebuttals to various theologians who attacked the Gospel I loved.

I grew in theological depth, but sometimes I wondered if I had plateaued in my *experience* of the Gospel. I had seen other ministers/ministries come to such a plateau in their own life. It's as if I was subconsciously saying, "I'm pretty happy here with what I know and with the theological *edge* that I can bring to a group of people." After all, the Bible study course I had written was being used as a training course for seasoned elders and pastors in churches from other states and even countries I'd never been to. Someone from Russia even asked my permission to translate my studies for use in their churches there. But was I growing in the realm of the kingdom, as far as greater authority and power in the things of the Spirit? Or was I following a common format of ministry and just following in the footsteps of so many others?

When's the last time you took a step back from all the commotion and religious activity to realistically see what your spiritual priorities really are? Not merely what you say they are from a theological standpoint, but what your time, use of money, resources, your immediate family, reflects. For example, someone could be considered successful in ministry (according to man's guidelines), but have a family undergoing serious issues because he or she has prioritized the applause of people over the applause of their own family. Someone else could be considered a mature church elder or deacon, because of his willingness to help at church each week, but the other six days of the week he compartmentalizes or restricts God to religious activities related to church, rather than Him being the source of everything he does on a daily basis.

Regardless of the list of priorities we each have concerning God, doctrines, and beliefs, I've found that *if* we truly take to heart the priority of things *in the order and way Jesus emphasized and said was most important*, God will empower us with His Spirit as promised. Outside of <u>His</u> order we're left with nothing more than the religious strivings of man that remain absent of God's endorsement of presence and power. *Kingdom order always attracts kingdom power and authority.* Just as the physical sanctuary in the Old Testament had a very specific *order* to house the presence of God, so in the New Testament, we are given living examples of a specific order for His new temple (us) to house His tangible presence and glory. I've seen and experienced firsthand, that as our beliefs align more and more with God's, the greater His power flows more and more unobstructed through us.

Matthew 22:35-40: [35] One of them, a lawyer, asked Him *a question*, testing Him, [36] "Teacher, which is the great commandment in the Law?" [37] And He said to him, "'YOU SHALL LOVE THE LORD YOUR GOD WITH ALL YOUR HEART, AND WITH ALL YOUR SOUL, AND WITH ALL YOUR MIND.' [38] This is the great and foremost commandment. [39] The second is like it, 'YOU SHALL LOVE YOUR NEIGHBOR AS YOURSELF.' [40] On these two commandments depend the whole Law and the Prophets.

Many of us can quote this very well, however *our practical life* shows the degree of importance we truly *believe* this to be. Notice I said, "practical life" not "intellectual or theological." My whole life, I understood faith or belief to be what doctrine or theology I *knew* in my mind. However, I've come to realize that definition is actually incorrect. I knew a lot through teachings and study, but believed very little in my heart, and this was confirmed by the lack of supernatural fruit and presence of God in my everyday life.

How we react to certain scenarios, what decisions we make, and the steps we apply to make them, how we spend our time, our money, and our resources reflects the actual degree of belief we truly have, despite what we may say theologically or intellectually to ourselves and one another. Our practical life activities are the fruits or manifestations, of what we actually believe. When a big crisis hits us or someone close to us, how we respond brings to surface our *practical belief*. For some, they'll turn to worry, fear, alcohol, food, social media, T.V. or other sources to cope with the crisis, because the crisis has challenged them beyond the level of their actual heart belief.

Our *practical life* clearly displays if we *truly* love God with *all* our heart, soul, and mind. Many modern-day churches emphasize what doctrines they *theologically* believe as the highest priority rather than the simple, yet profound, truth Jesus tells the lawyer in that verse. It's common to hear, "As for the practical side of things and how we live the other six days of the week, it's a hit or miss kind of thing we all struggle through life with. But, as long as you have those doctrines intact *in your head*, that is what's most important." This same mindset was seen numerous times in the New Testament religious leaders, even immediately following the raw power and presence of God, demonstrated through a miracle made manifest by Jesus. These religious leaders would ask Jesus a question about a particular doctrine *they felt was more important* than what Jesus had just done (Jn 5:1-17) *showing they valued their list of priorities more over Jesus'*.

Misaligned priorities can cause us to also miss Him every time, as all we'll focus on is the difference of priority of that doctrine rather than *what He is bringing about*. But the raw presence and power of God exposes the reality of God in a *practical way* that sheds light on the shallowness of modern-day religion, and causes people to either receive the living reality being displayed or retreat to what insulates their plateaued state of religiosity, just as the Pharisees did. Romans 7:15 ("What I want to do I don't do and what I don't want to do I do...") is often misquoted in many religious circles to try and cover a multitude of spiritual immature behavior and inadequacies that only the pure, practical Gospel could fix. I know many religious circles that believe the devil's *main* plan of attack toward their set of doctrines. So, they heavily emphasize "*you* need to always keep our doctrines intact in your head and stay away from anything challenging *them* because it is an attack from the devil."

But His attack isn't on *them* (your intellectual belief) but on you. Remember, as long as our theological and intellectual system of beliefs isn't producing the supernatural fruit – that only comes from God's tangible presence and voice – the devil couldn't care less. As far as he's concerned, we can co-labor with any powerless manmade ministry or church as long as we're not co-laboring with the ministry of Jesus Christ – the anointed-smeared with God. In fact, he'll even help convince us to be satisfied with how smart and enlightened we've become. He'll encourage us to compare ourselves to so many other Christians, because as long as *we* think we're in a state of "rich, having increased with goods, and wanting for nothing," and other people believing the same, we'll fail to realize just how wretched and miserable and poor and blind and naked we really are, according to Jesus' assessment of this last day church (Rev.3:17-20).

While I know Satan operates by suggesting and encouraging lies, remember any and every deception has one thing in mind: separating you and me from God's presence and voice – the practical experiencing of God, not merely our shallow, mental understanding *about* Him. Practically loving God with our everything and loving our neighbor, as Jesus mentioned in this text, is of utmost highest priority *above* any and everything else, according to Jesus's highest priority, not man's.

You can feel, see, hear, and experience a drastic difference from people who seek *above all else* to love God like this verse describes, compared to those whose *practical* life testifies of a very divided heart, soul, and mind. It's the major differentiating factor between the religious spirit displayed in the Pharisees of Jesus' day and the spirituality displayed in the life of Jesus and the disciples who followed Him. One is an open landing pad for the Spirit of God to embody, speak through and move through, where the other is not.

"The light of the body is the eye: **if** therefore thine eye be **single**, thy whole body shall be *full* of light."-Mat.6:22. Note: "Single, undivided, wholly focused eye..." not a divided, partial, *when convenient* I'll do it, eye.

Think about this for a moment: How long can you currently spend with God before you get bored? Before you get uncomfortable? Distracted? ten minutes, twenty, or thirty? Lovers have no problem being together and enjoying life with one another. In fact, *time is most often forgotten in the presence of one we are truly in love with*. When we are truly becoming more aligned with the priorities and agenda of heaven instead of man's, you'll find that time apart from His presence becomes more and more unbearable and a growing ache deep inside of you longing to be with Him more than ever before. You'll find your own life's priorities deciding how you spend your time, energies, or money, shifting to greater and greater degrees for the purpose of just being with Him and being more fully *His*. You'll find yourself sacrificing things that once were dear to you, but now seemingly worthless in comparison to the experiential bliss of His person. It's the practical experience Paul described in Philippians 3:7-10, when he said, "I'd count it all rubbish that I may win Christ."

So, the question that can typically follow is, "*How* can I get my eye to be single or *only fixed* on Him?" *How* can I learn to love the Lord with all my heart, soul, and mind? Well, there's God's way, which is extremely effective, and man's way which isn't. All throughout Scripture, you will see both contrasted, especially when looking at the Old and New Covenants of Scripture. The word *covenant* when used in the Bible is similar to the word *contract* today. You'll find several kinds of covenants – or contracts – in the Old Testament between God and man, and one final covenant in the New Testament called the New Covenant.

The covenants from the Old Testament (especially the one between God and the people of Israel) are referred to as the Old Covenant, or *first covenant*; whereas the New Covenant in the New Testament is referred to as the *second covenant*. We will cover more about these in later chapters, but it's important to know that Jesus died to usher in the New Covenant which was *vitally needed* and unmatched by any covenants/contracts prior to Jesus. Scripture says,

"...if that first covenant had been faultless, then should no place have been sought for the second." -Heb.8:7 NKJV.

The major difference between the Old vs. New, is in the Old Covenant, man's understanding and practical experience of purity, holiness, and sanctification, was limited to the mere *external* disciplining and abstaining of one's *physical self or body* from sin. That's why if you read the Old Testament books, specifically Exodus, Deuteronomy, and Leviticus, there is a heavy emphasis on the *external abstaining* from sin or things unclean. The abstaining from kept the people very *sin conscious* as this was *how* they were instructed to remain clean. Jesus hadn't died yet, our sins had not legally been forgiven, and therefore, we were unable to house the presence of the living God inside of us.

So, without His indwelling presence, man carried out many sacrificial, ceremonial, and traditional activity to *signify* the cleansing of their sin in the Old Testament, although *there was no actual transformation taking place*. This verse touches on that very point:

But in those *sacrifices there is* a reminder of sins every year. ⁴For *it is not possible that the blood of bulls and goats could take away sins.*" -Hebrews 10:3,4 NKJV.

In other words, they were carrying out an *activity that was actually powerless to change them*. An intellectual acknowledgement of one thing while the *practical life completely unaltered*. This is as far as man can operate, apart from the indwelling presence of God, remaining *sin conscious* year after year always ashamed, guilty, defeated by the devil, while *intellectually and theologically* acknowledging certain teachings and carrying out certain religious traditions *apart* from true victory, transformation, freedom, of the indwelling presence of God.

If we fall prey to such a powerless religious application today, we are operating under a covenant or system that is in direct opposition of everything the cross has victoriously defeated for us. It's as if He'd never came and died for us. Hence, why this "religious spirit," prevalent in Jesus' day and in ours, is so extremely deceptive, and an utterly nauseating disgust to Jesus as He says in Rev. 3:16: it makes Him want to vomit. What could be worse than a people claiming to know, be with, and have inside of them the *living Christ Jesus,* and yet not look like, talk like, or behave like Him? It's a testament to the world that He must not be real, alive, practical, tangible, or as good as we claim with our *words* and *theology*. It's the epitome of the church, which was described in the first chapter, with polished programs but little to no tangible liberating power or presence of Jesus.

Jesus prayed something very special right before He was taken to the cross:

> [20] "I do not pray for these alone, but also for those who will believe in Me through their word; [21] that they *all may be* one, *as You, Father, are in Me, and I in You; that they also may be one in Us, that the world may believe that You sent Me.* -John 17:20,21 NKJV

Religion says the oneness Jesus is praying for here, is oneness in the theological doctrine we agree on, and that the devil cares most to attack our doctrines more than anything else. But in the Old Covenant, there was even more of an abundance of theological agreeance and specifics beyond any denomination today (over 600+ laws/doctrine), and yet all their agreements couldn't bring about the oneness with Jesus and the Father described here.

Jesus could have easily taught us the correct doctrines we should agree on, and not have to die, but He came so that we could each experience something much deeper, more practical, and real: God Himself, indwelling and imparting Himself, His presence, into mortal man.

"Do you not know that you are the temple of God and *that* the Spirit of God dwells in you?" -1Cor.3:16 NKJV. Did you catch that? In the Old Testament, God's presence was in the most Holy place, in the physical sanctuary, accessed only by one High Priest once a year. But, when Jesus was birthed on this planet, God's presence then dwelled in Him through the Holy Spirit, and therefore, wherever Jesus went you could *directly* access the presence and power of God in Him, hence the verse declaring Jesus was "God with us" (Mat. 1:23).

But, by His death, He defeated sin so that *just as* He carried the presence and modeled what the life of a redeemed son or daughter of the most high would look like, we too, would receive our restored status and become the very temple/dwelling place of God.

> *In the New Covenant, the key difference isn't a set of moral codes, doctrine, or instruction. It's the*

restoration of the image and likeness of God by the indwelling presence of God the Holy Spirit in us.

The Holy Spirit is so vital that, even after walking with, living with, and hearing Jesus for three and a half years, the disciples were instructed to *wait* for this indwelling of God, the Holy Spirit, *before* carrying out their mission to tell the world about Jesus. (Acts 1:4,5).

Their intellectual knowledge *about* Him, even their *past stories* of actual experiences walking with Him on earth was still not enough to qualify them for their redeemed purpose in life or ministry. Remember, even the religious leaders had *past experiences* they'd clung to, in exchange for the *present experiencing of Jesus,* who physically stood with them. *Only His empowering present presence can set us apart unto holiness.* This is the heart of a spiritual, New Covenant, "Loving the Lord with our all," kind of life. Oh, that we would realize how simple, restful, this life is, when we realize, "in His presence there is *fullness* of joy." (Ps.16:11). *You and I are currently experiencing whatever degree of rest and joy that correlates to the degree of His presence we have experientially received and choose to live life with.* So, if we're settling to live 90% of our daily activity apart from His presence, we'll continue to only experience 10% of the rest, joy, and peace He died for. But if a man or woman truly dies to themselves, resigns their former way of thinking and lies of unbelief, and allows Jesus to completely be Lord of *all*, the bliss of heaven is what is experienced, even while still being in the midst of a sinful world, (Jn17:3).

I believe most every Christian can recall their first experience of God's presence touching their heart. For a moment, can you remember that time He first touched you? When your heart was thumping out of your chest as you felt His presence asking if He could come into your life? It could have been at an altar call at church, Bible study, club, party, bar, alley, car, or anywhere else. But the touch was so real and powerful that it conveyed more about the existence of God's presence than the world had about a life of sin. But it's also common to hear *seasoned* Christians refer to that touch as "first love." They'll say things like, "Yeah, I remember what that was like... I was just so excited to tell people about Jesus and my newfound faith in Him, that I couldn't shut up about it. But then, reality came back and life continued."

As with my own experience, many of us were truly touched by His presence to the degree that the most obvious outward sins were surrendered up to Him. In my case, it was the weed smoking, partying, drinking, and all that goes with that lifestyle. But then what happened to so many of us, is the devil comes and said, *"Okay, so you want to get religious, huh? Let me show you what this is all about and what it looks like to be a church-going Christian."*

He then tries to isolate that real, tangible, touch we had of God's presence as a "once in a lifetime" experience, so that we settle for a powerless religious form from that point on. We eventually assimilate the very predictable, molded lifestyle of the religious leaders or teachers we listen to week after week at church, and our ceiling of supernatural expectancy (which was so high after our first encounter with Him) shatters and is lowered to the mere reasoning of man.

We are theologically and practically taught right into unbelief and out of the childlike, pure, belief that He provoked us with in the beginning of our experience of Him. We learn how to explain away the obvious lack of supernatural activity just as our leaders have, and since everyone else who is more mature in the faith has done it for decades, then why would we care to believe or expect anything more? In fact, the religious culture portrays this question as *selfish* since, "You should *learn* how be satisfied with just studying your Bible like everyone else does."

"Blessed are the pure in heart, for they will see God..." Mat 5:8. The word *see* here isn't merely with physical eyes but is meant to perceive God and His presence in multiple ways. When I believed in a one-time-touch kind of Gospel, I had severed myself from a *lifestyle* of God's presence being the center of my spirituality, since I only had a *monument from my past* that I could only look back to, "that time I experienced Him so real." Like many of us, that one touch was sufficient to take care of numerous outward sins, but how far could it take us before the cleansing would stop? We went from tasting the New Covenant reality of God changing us by His Supernatural presence, back into the Old Covenant methods... of a lot of religious activity, church programs, and Bible study for our intellect. It's like we subconsciously realize, *"Okay, God took care of the big sins, but now it's time for you to get serious like the rest of the mature believers..."*

We eventually believe that the most significant change has already taken place in our lives, comparing the sins of our pasts to the present. But it is the devil's deception that keeps us from experiencing the tangible presence of God on a daily basis, because His presence alone brings about a pure heart and the spiritual clarity to really see and experience Him like the verse above (Matt. 5:8) says.

Just like an ideal relationship between a husband and wife, intimacy with God is the byproduct of greater and greater transparency, truth, and very real conversations, communication, and time together. This begins with God first, but then it permeates into every personal relationship we have.

As my expectancy and belief of His tangible presence and power has increased, so has an effortless and accelerated cleansing of my heart, in the same fashion as He did in the beginning, when He first touched me. Except now, it's character flaws, weaknesses, critical judgmental habits/perspectives, self-righteousness, pride, religious pride, husband pride, arrogance, and many other things that were never challenged and transformed with a lifetime of "nominal one-touch religion." It's all the behind closed doors thoughts and conversations stuff that religion is so efficient at hiding and condoning, since the main focus of religion is on the outward – how we look, what we say, and what we do, rather than who we really are when nobody is looking or listening.

His presence is truly life and, apart from it, we're left with powerless religion and a false perception of God and our own spiritual lives. His presence will not only radically change your relationship with Him as it becomes more genuine and real, but that same genuineness and authenticity will change how you see and treat every person, change every relationship you have with your spouse, family, friends, and even strangers.

"I am the way, and the truth, and the life; no one comes to the Father but through Me." Jn 14:6 NASB. I heard someone say, "Jesus Christ is perfect theology," and I couldn't agree more. After all He is THE way, THE truth, THE life and the means of how we have gained access into the Father's presence. I promise Jesus is truly enough. Whatever part of you feels the need to add a "Yeah but…" to that, is most likely an indication that you just haven't experienced Him in the deep, all satisfying, intimacies He invites us all to.

But now you can, as you respond to His pull and receive Him into your heart, right now.

I invite you to take an intellectual break from reading this, even for just thirty seconds... I believe God has led you to this very point, because He wants to provoke you to a life filled with His tangible voice and presence. A life where you're not merely surviving, but one of living victoriously over anyone and everything that comes at you. Before we say this prayer, I want to raise your expectancy for what *may likely* happen to you in this prayer. In later chapters, we will discuss some of the tangible ways God's presence can be physically sensed/felt.

Now, as we pray, I want you to simply be aware of any of the following possible things that you *may* experience during this prayer: heat on your head and/or body, tingling, (similar to when your arm/leg has fallen asleep) trembling, overwhelming sense of peace, and/or a sense of divine peace and stillness.

I know, you're probably saying to yourself, "Is he for real? Is this getting to new age stuff now?" But as you keep reading, seeing from scripture, and experiencing Him for yourself, you'll see this confirmed over and over. God is a consuming fire, and the Holy Spirit is truly a real tangible person of the Godhead that can be sensed beyond head knowledge. Like me, you probably just never realized how often you have sensed Him because nobody around you knew how to. Physical manifestations aren't necessarily a must to affirm He is here with you. He is here, whether you feel it or not because He said He is. But we've also gone to the other extreme with that, an all-out of fear of being "feelings based" and "deceived." You do not need to muster anything up in your own strength or fake it. He doesn't need your help to *do* anything. Just rest and receive. Just be *neutral* to receiving however God wants you to encounter Him right now, as it's His desire to build your faith in His ways, as you pray:

"Jesus, I want to receive more of your living presence in my life. I want the eyes of my heart to be opened to see the mysteries of Your person in ways that provoke me for more of You. Holy Spirit, make me aware of your tangible presence right now... (now close your eyes and simply wait about a minute in surrendered silence to see if you notice His presence touching you in any way physically or internally). Holy Spirit, show me how to let You lead instead of using my human

intellect to try and understand the infinite God of the universe. In Jesus' name, Amen.

Jesus never said, "I know the way" but rather, "I am the way." If He had said, "I know the way," we could merely take what intellectual and theological information He knows from Him and once obtaining the formula, go on our way to live apart from Him. This theory applies to most modern religious organizations today. But, *because He is THE way, it is impossible to be truly following Him apart from the ongoing experiencing of His presence.* Hence, why we are taking this time to examine "the Way" Jesus practically modeled His life. The keys to unlocking our spiritual potential, making full effect of the cross in our own experience, is found in following Jesus. I know we've all heard and said that phrase a billion times, but I pray as we're looking at His life now, we'll come to grips of what "following Him" *really* means.

To understand more fully what following Jesus truly means, we can simply look to *the way* Jesus followed the leading of His Father through the Holy Spirit's presence.

> "...Most assuredly, I say to you, the Son can do nothing of Himself, but *what He sees* the Father do; for whatever He does, the Son also does in like manner. [20] For the Father loves the Son, and shows Him all things that He Himself does; and He will show Him greater works than these, that you may marvel. John 5:19-20 NKJV

Romans 8:16,17 makes it very clear that we are "joint heirs" or "joint inheritors" with Jesus. And, as a result, His rights as a "son" or "child" of God, are now ours. Hence, why the "Holy Spirit is *constantly* bearing witness in our spirits that we are children of God." (vs. 16). In other words, Holy Spirit is always bringing us into the living, practical reality of the life of the Son of God because it's that very life He died to give us. So, in Jn. 5:19-20, Jesus is showing us by example "the way" a son/daughter of God is to live: "Do nothing of (originating) from yourself. What you *see* (experientially-not just intellectually or theologically) the Father do, do that. Because the Father loves the son (you) and shows (present tense) Him all things that He Himself

31

does, and He will show Him greater works than these (the miracle He had just done) that you may marvel."

Notice *a son or daughter of God sets their life to a present tense experiencing of God's presence, seeing what the Father is doing, and receiving fresh living revelation from what the Father is presently showing us.* Jesus never had to rely on stale revelation from last week, because He was always in tune with what His Father was *presently* doing and seeing in whatever scenario, circumstance, or situation He'd walked into at the moment. And this is precisely the difference between one who believes their redeemed identity as a son or daughter of God and one who doesn't.

Do you believe the God of heaven has truly restored you, not as a slave, not as a church goer, not as one who merely now abstains from things you once did, but as a literal son or daughter of the living God? What is your first reaction if you closed your eyes and prayed saying, "Daddy?" Do you feel like you're being irreverent? Too child-like maybe? Do you get instantly uncomfortable? "[15] For you did not receive the spirit of bondage again to fear, but you received the Spirit of adoption by whom we cry out, "Abba (Daddy), Father." (Ro.8:15). Believe it. Holy Spirit is inviting you to truly receive your restored identity as "son or daughter of the living God," so that you can begin to follow Him in a whole new adventurous way. Jesus shows us the Father's heart is to be *continually* leading us from a constant experiencing of His tangible presence and voice. If we embrace the crippling lies of the religious spirit, we'll settle for a predictable, dry, powerless, life, that only has interest in reciting what God *once said and once did* rather than believing He wants to bring you in much closer to Himself and actually show you what He is doing and what He is saying in direct correlation to your present life and world.

When we view the Scriptures as a ceiling rather than a springboard, we'll always be looking for ways to take something out of them and apply it to our present circumstance, as if God is only interested in speaking to us indirectly. It's such a lie. Of course, the enemy wants us to settle for indirect communication. Nothing creates distance in a relationship like severing off the actual tangible time spent talking with and being with someone. It's like we believe Him to be that Dad who's never home with us, spending time with us, or even speaking to us directly, but instead just sends us letters in the mail that we just reread over and over, because eventually He stopped writing and sending those too.

> [49] For I have not spoken on My own *authority;* but the Father who sent Me gave Me a command, what I should say and what I should speak. John 12:49 NKJV.

Jesus here, once again, showing that *all*, not just some, or most, but *all* of His words and actions originated *only* from the authority of the Father who sent Him.

How does a son or daughter of the living God get to a point of completely surrendering to the will, voice, and authority of God? How does a person like you or me become so in tune with our Father in heaven that we are now His voice and body on the earth? After all, Jesus calls His church *His body*. Well, the same Spirit of the living God that possessed Jesus *now* seeks for another "body" to fill, possess, empower and relay the voice and will of the living God in tangible form and expression through us. Hence, why living a life that is "presence centered" and seeking to hear what He IS saying today, is such a threat to the enemy. Instead of one physical body possessed by the Spirit of God, now there can be millions. (Heb.2:10). Millions of God's children who are carrying out their family (God's family) business, namely, showing the lost just how loved they really are by their heavenly Father. This supernatural love is best demonstrated like Jesus did-healing the sick, raising the dead, casting out demons etc. Notice, all of these demonstrations are supernatural reflecting where it comes from.

Sickness, disease, and death itself surrenders to any son/daughter who truly believes and lives from their redeemed identity and authority of the New Covenant gospel. Jesus is our only example of how a "son/daughter" should pray, as He commanded the sick to be healed, the dead to be raised, etc. He is the only person in the books of Matthew, Mark, Luke, and John that a New Covenant believer should be identifying with. The many books of the New Testament are very clear in declaring our redeemed authority to be expressed and demonstrated *just as Jesus modeled*. He never prayed from the position of a servant, begging God to heal someone like so many of us have done. Although sincere, that rarely "works" because it is not aligned with the New Covenant truths of the completed gospel. Instead such "begging" demonstrates we are still operating under the powerless Old Covenant and don't believe we've been given such authority and power already as redeemed *sons*. But Jesus commanded sickness to leave as a divine son should. The more our minds are renewed to these New Covenant realities, the more supernatural fruit follow us, affirming we are co-laboring with Jesus as fellow "joint heirs."

Throughout the book you will hear me mention New Covenant "Identity" as being one of the first things God began to help me with (and still does). I will also share several resources regarding identity that have helped me identify areas in my thinking and heart that needed to be renewed to New Covenant truth in order to allow New Covenant power to come out from me.

The truth of New Covenant identity removes hindrances in our minds so that His power/Spirit can flow out of us with miraculous fruit.

While relationship with Holy Spirit-hearing His voice and learning His ways, allows us to be one with His heart so that His character is also displayed with that divine authority and power.

Demonstrating divine power is amazing, but also enjoying the New Covenant experiences of God's presence and voice unlike any other previous era of time is equally just as incredible. Together, His power and character of love are reflected through us and are unstoppable. It is our redeemed inheritance as sons/daughters to enjoy it all.

I invite you to pray this prayer from your heart:

Father, help me to understand even that very word "Father" beyond what I have experienced from my earthly Father... Help me to believe your love, follow through, provisions, and words are always true, always constant, and never failing. Help me to truly receive and believe that Jesus' blood has truly been enough of a price, to give me such an inheritance as a son/daughter of the living God, despite what things I've done or not done. Help me to truly believe in the great magnitude of miraculous, supernatural power, presence, and provision You have called me to become the very expression of in my daily life, as I'm more and more indwelt with Holy Spirit. Help me to become more aware of Your tangible presence today, in Jesus' name, Amen.

CHAPTER 4

HOLY SPIRIT LEADS

I remember when my wife and I had just left a church that we had helped plant and co-pastor for several years. I felt like God was being so slow to lead us to the next church or ministry He wanted us to "do ministry in" like I'd done for almost a decade.

I remember telling my friend, "I just don't know what God wants me doing right now. I'm feeling the itch to teach and preach, but don't know where God wants us."

The reality was I understood teaching and preaching to be ministry in and of themselves and a large part of my Christian identity. I remember my personal time with the Lord back then would fluctuate often, with the peak being ten to twenty minutes a day, plus time to prepare a sermon to preach that week and maybe giving a Bible study or teaching a Bible class. This was actually "pretty good," in my own estimation as I'd subconsciously compare myself to those around me and felt I was doing just fine in the area of time with God. Then my friend said something that became a pivotal turning point to the false spiritual assessment I held of myself:

> "What if God doesn't want you doing formal ministry right now, but instead becoming the ministry? What if He's saying, "Okay, you've functioned in the formal spotlight of ministry but will you let me have all the other time instead?""

What he was saying made sense in theory and the correct thing to say, but I didn't quite understand it practically, so he told me of some things that really stirred my hunger to wanting more of God to possess my practical life. One of the few things he shared was a testimony he'd recently heard from a person named Todd White (*www.*

Lifestylechristianity.com). I had never heard of him and, as usual, I was very skeptical since he wasn't from my denomination and there-fore, in my mind, "not as knowledgeable of the truth as I was." But what my friend was describing sounded too good to be true. So, I watched a YouTube video of a powerful testimony in which Todd was *being the ministry* empowered by the Holy Spirit in his day-to-day life. He loved people through practical and supernatural means and expressed it to them in ways I'd only heard of Jesus and the early church doing. I was instantly stirred with conviction that God had so much more for me to experience. I longed to know my Jesus in such a way He could possess me *how He pleased whenever He pleased.* Although I still wanted to learn more about Todd's beliefs and doc-trine to see if he passed my "theological deception-free checklist," I prayerfully proceeded to ask God, "God, are you actually doing the supernatural things I've only read about, even today? Are you still supernaturally healing, delivering, resurrecting, performing signs and wonders today? If so, I want to know *where* you're doing these things and *why,* so that I can be a part of what you're *currently* doing."

And this is where my adventure into a Spirit-led life began. There God challenged me to devote my all to Him in a fresh surrender of Him truly being Lord, not merely of my theology and doctrine, but of my practical life, my time, money, hobbies, and so much more. As Mark Batterson once said, "If He isn't Lord of all, He isn't Lord at all." I had known Jesus as my Savior but not Lord. Up to this point, my life had clearly reflected just that.

Does this resonate at all with you? Perhaps some similarity to where you are now in your relationship with Jesus? Maybe you're not who you once were, when you were in the world, but could it be He is yearning for an even *more full* surrender to Him, as your Lord? Something beyond that *one touch* from long ago? He wants an even *greater* degree of entrusting yourself to Him and His pres-ence than ever before. Could it be what your church, friends, and family would consider extreme or fanatical devotion to Jesus, is exactly what stands between your present experience and one that is overflowing with the supernatural presence and power of God? A life where His presence is radiating from every word you say and everything you do is his desire for you. Could it be He wants to oblit-erate the current segregated areas of your life? Those segregated areas like: church time, God time, movie time, T.V. time, friends time, secular music time, can be merged so that His presence becomes the *center* from which everything, and I mean *everything* flows from.

I can tell you this, I've now seen more ministries, individuals, and places where the tangible presence and power of God are clearly operating as in Scripture... more than I can count. At the core of every authentic one, I've found there to be no less surrender to Him than absolute. The veil to the most holy place of the God of the universe *was* torn open for us to *now* approach Him with boldness (Heb.10:19,20). Therefore, our practical life has no excuse to look like one that is still *waiting* on God to give us access to such presence. To do so is to deny Jesus the very fruit He died to see produced in us, namely His presence to *now* live, dwell, abide, and remain in us 24/7. I truly believe that we can have as much of Him as *we want* and we are currently experiencing exactly that. We may say one thing with our words, "Lord we want more of you, we want your Holy Spirit to fall on us," but the Lord looks at our hearts and unfortunately, one thing may lack a complete, and full "Yes" to His reign and Lordship as He would have it.

God is a God of power and *demonstrative* love. He loves to teach us by bringing us into real living examples and encounters with truth personally and from the lives of others. It's the difference between walking away with a greater intellect of something versus walking away transformed. But if we only drink from the same dead pond we can't expect to receive anything less than the same bacteria we've grown accustomed to. What I mean is, if the people we look up to in church, we listen to from week to week, and read from, don't have the supernatural fruit that was/is demonstrated in each disciple/apostle of the living Christ, then it's very possible God is more fully using people outside of that pond and from other streams of *living* water. The sobering reality is our fruit simply reflects the substance or lack within us and nothing more. I can't give you a greater quality of supernatural fruit from my "tree" than what I, myself, am walking in or believing in. I can speak *about* a lot of things from a head-knowledge standpoint, but its power and influence pale in comparison to the fruit that comes out, overflowing from my living experience with Holy Spirit, which has power to transform.

Long ago, I had skepticism of any person or ministry with any greater degree of Holy Spirit displaying in their life than what I was used to. But perhaps the reason we are so quick to label someone or something as "demonic" or "deception" is because we are truly too lazy to test it in our own practical lives. If someone told you, "I started to spend three-plus hours per morning with the Lord, and then I began to experience visions, dreams, encounters with angels, and seeing miracles," how can you test this? Do you just try and find some doctrine this person teaches that is contrary to what you believe and label them, based on a group that believes like them, and then disregard them? Well that's what I used to do. I used to use my extensive theological background to figure out what things this person believes, or not, so that I could say, "Oh they teach this or that *false doctrine,* which came from that denomination or person, which is deception." In fact, I became very good at quickly finding the deception or differences from my (self-labeled) pure theological truths and slapped a label on them without batting an eyelash.

However, despite how widely practiced such fleshly discernment is practiced abroad in the church today, it's the spirit of religion and it has always operated like this (many examples of Pharisees doing precisely this to Jesus) but it's truly spiritual laziness and immaturity. I've seen countless ministries, individuals, and pastors labeled just like this and what's even sadder is the *many* members of the church who were just as lazy to believe the label someone else told them about that person or ministry group, rather than actually taking the prayerful time with the Lord and with that person or ministry group to make a more personal and accurate assessment. People can make their whole life's calling and emphasis on critiquing other ministries "in the name of God" rather than letting God build something new, fresh, and alive through their own life.

I know the fear of being deceived often prevented me from wanting to explore anything different or outside of what I believed was safe. But, really, it was a big insecurity and unbelief I had in the Holy Spirit's ability to guide me to *all* truth. When our security of truth is based on "how intact can I keep my theological understanding from wavering?" we are relying on ourselves and our mental and theological energies to keep us from being led astray, rather than relying on the actual relationship and leading of Holy Spirit. Jesus said, "I am the truth," not "I have the truth," as His emphasis was this: our degree of truth is always contingent to the degree of His presence is present in our practical lives-rather than just a shallow mental acknowledgement of a set of doctrines. Christ's method and instruction always pointed us to rely on the divine *person* Holy Spirit as He refers to Him as the very "guide to *all* truth," and nothing less. When we *practically* believe and *act* from Him in His proper role, we can *fearlessly* explore places, people, and things, as our confidence is no longer in ourselves or our own carnal abilities but in relationship and leading from Him.

So much of the church body is stuck in the fear of being led astray and, as a result, contained in a false security bubble which never guides them to the path of God's current activity. In such a false security bubble, there's little to no need for a guide such as the Holy Spirit. A guide is only needed to explore unfamiliar territory such as the inexhaustible supernatural, spiritual realm of God.

If someone told you that you needed to start using a guide or GPS to help you navigate through your own neighborhood each day, you'd laugh at the thought, since you're so acquainted with the way and have no need of directional help. Insert: the false securities of religious systems today. When we buy into the humanly constructed, familiar, explainable, predictable systems of religion, we practically find little to any need for a growing understanding of Holy Spirit's present tense voice in our lives, since everything we are operating in has become extremely predictable, explainable and familiar to us. For anything else that we'd rather leave until later, (as if our access to such things is still denied), we recite this first part of 1 Corinthians 2:9 saying,

> "THINGS WHICH EYE HAS NOT SEEN AND EAR HAS NOT HEARD, AND *which* HAVE NOT ENTERED THE HEART OF MAN, ALL THAT GOD HAS PREPARED FOR THOSE WHO LOVE HIM."

But we don't realize how often we misquote that scripture. If you read further, the passage continues elaborating on the *present* reality of the believer that no longer lives out of synch with the supernatural realm as in the Old Covenant era (where that text is quoted from). Watch in this next verse what Paul says is our inheritance to live out *now, today, if* we embrace the spiritual life Jesus died to give us over the spirit*less* lies of religiosity:

[10] "For to us God revealed *them (what eye had not seen, ear heard etc.) through the Spirit*; for the Spirit searches all things, even the depths of God. [11] For who among men knows the *thoughts* of a man except the spirit of the man which is in him? Even so the *thoughts* of God no one knows except the Spirit of God. [12] Now we have received, not the spirit of the world, but the Spirit who is from God, *so that we may know the things freely given to us by God*, [13] which things we also speak, *not* in words taught by human wisdom, but in those taught by the Spirit, combining spiritual *thoughts* with spiritual *words*.[14] But a natural man does not accept the things of the Spirit of God, for they are foolishness to him; and he cannot understand them, because they are spiritually appraised."

Paul, the apostle and writer of this passage is elaborating on the raw reality that only one *person* (not one doctrine, one formula, or one denomination) is qualified to be our guide into the spiritual, experiential relationship with God, and it's the "Spirit who searches the depths of God... and knows the thoughts of God." Hence, why there's only one unpardonable sin mentioned in the New Testament: blaspheming the Holy Spirit, because rejecting an experiential, present tense, relationship with Him is to reject an experiential, supernatural, intimate relationship with God Himself (Matthew 12:31-32). God didn't just redeem us so He could, one day, transport us to a physical place called *Heaven*. He redeemed us to restore the practical union with Him in which every cell in our bodies has been crying out for since the moment we fell out of synch with His reality. Our proximity and depth of experiencing Holy Spirit tangibly in our lives today is of utmost and vital importance to actually knowing (ongoing) the voice and presence of God. Hence, why the enemy seeks to sell us any and every counterfeit to this reality, especially the spirit of religiosity which has worked so effectively to deceive others in the past.

A sense of childlike adventure began to grow in me as I ventured to believe God for His promised leading through the Holy Spirit, above all my previous methods. Would I soon stumble into the same encounters, experiences, and joys of the supernatural realm of God as I'd only read about in scripture? Could this reality be the missing link that God had been yearning to bring me into so that I could begin to live a more abundant life? Well, I was now beginning to hear and be faced with present-day testimonies, experiences, encounters, miracles, signs and wonders from people and places outside of my bubble. I was being stretched into areas that were foreign to my practical experience. But such scenarios make a perfect setup for needing intimacy with Holy Spirit more than ever before. It's in this very adventure of exploring the supernatural ways of God that I've grown so much closer to the Holy Spirit. I'd be so clueless without Him.

If you'd asked me before, "Hey do you believe God can heal today?" I would have told you "Of course. He's the same yesterday, today, and forever." I would have also said, "I'm sure it's happening in third-world countries somewhere... but not here in the US." But if I heard you pray for someone with the redeemed authority that we've now been given over sickness and disease and then I actually saw the person healed as a result, I would have been instantly challenged with many questions in my own practical relationship with God.

But over time I've learned to respond to supernatural testimonies saying, "God, if this fruit really is from you, then I too, can begin to tap into such supernatural things *if* I begin to practically place my priorities more in alignment with Biblical truth." In other words, I can't reject someone's supernatural fruit because it's different than mine, if at their root is a much more intimate relationship with God and truth, than mine. As a result, I began to personally see and experience more and more supernatural signs, wonders, miracles, and encounters in my life – from Angelic activity to dreams and visions, to the overwhelming presence of Jesus Himself. But it truly is all a *natural* byproduct of intimacy with Him. Nothing more and nothing less.

It's important to know, that there are counterfeits of the supernatural works of God. Some are demonic works or manifestations,

41

some the flesh (a person pretending), and others spiritual gifts from God that men eventually continued to carry out without intimacy with God. ("For God's gifts and His call can never be withdrawn." -Romans 11:29 NLT.)

Often, when a man/woman is operating purely out of his/her gifting rather than intimacy with God, their characters show pride, ego, self-righteousness, or even more obvious contradictions to God's character. This is a major stumbling block, especially if we're already coming from a place of skepticism.

> [21] Not everyone who says to Me, 'Lord, Lord,' will enter the kingdom of heaven, but he who does the will of My Father who is in heaven *will enter*. [22] Many will say to Me on that day, 'Lord, Lord, did we not prophesy in Your name, and in Your name cast out demons, and in Your name perform many miracles?' [23] And then I will declare to them, *'I never knew you*; DEPART FROM ME, YOU WHO PRACTICE LAWLESSNESS.' MATTHEW 7:21-23 NASB.

I didn't want to be led astray from truth by an external wonder and then wander away from God. But, like many other Christians, I allowed such fears to evolve into pure unbelief of the authentic supernatural works of God. I had learned and taught religious theologies rooted in unbelief and skepticism, in exchange for the supernatural presence and fruit of God. Looking back, I see such beliefs of unbelief were a false sense of religious security, rather than biblical truths.

Public supernatural works, no matter how magnificent, are unimpressive to God if they are not the by-product of genuine time spent with Him in *private*. It's out of such intimacy with Him, that He changes our characters and hearts to become the divine substance of unconditional love He has shown to us. Apart from such genuine love, it's all meaningless.

In our next chapter we'll uncover the practical applications of this Biblical root, which must *always* be prioritized in our hearts and characters if we want to follow the authentic path Jesus has invited us into.

CHAPTER 5

HIS SECRETS IN THE SECRET PLACE

Multiple generations of family members gathered together for a special family reunion day. The day had been filled with games, laughter, tons of food, and good times together. The smell of freshly grilled chicken, steak, and hot dogs filled the air. Then all of a sudden, Uncle John collapsed to the ground and appeared to be completely lifeless, without any breath or movement.

"Uncle John fell down!" one of the kids screamed. You would have thought this would send the surrounding adult family members into a desperate panic, crying for help, but instead they quickly formed a circle around his lifeless body. Several debates began.

Someone said, "Well, we'll have to change those clothes into something more formal because what he has on now is embarrassing..."

Another person said, "I think we should shave his beard down to how it was when we were growing up."

Another rebutted, "No, absolutely not. It needs to stay the way it is now."

The debates continued with what each person believed should be done or not to Uncle John's body for an open casket viewing. Finally, after about ten minutes of this, a family member who had been in the restroom walked up and saw Uncle John laying there.

"He needs CPR. Nothing else matters right now except that Uncle John is revived back to life." And as she said this, everyone quickly realized that although there were many differences of opinions among them, they needed to set those aside at the moment, and unite for the sole purpose of bringing Uncle John back to life. And so, they ceased the debating and decided to unite for the same, one, purpose: revive Uncle John.

Over the past hundred-plus years, there has been more separating divisions in the body of Christ (His Church) unlike anything ever witnessed before. There are currently well over three-hundred-plus Christian denominations that each have their emphasis on certain aspects of scriptures that differ from the others. In the early church, saying you were a Christian was the only label identifying New Covenant believers, since the name *Christ* was identified as the very substance, center, and focal-point of what their life was centered around.

However, today we are faced with various man-made religions, endorsed by man, and honored by man, and prided with an arrogance that may be convincing to ourselves and a handful of others, but is completely and utterly nauseating to Jesus. He desires to exchange our manmade trophies for a reviving of His Spirit back into His body, *the church*. We have so many opinions of what the Word of God says, but if those doctrines simply "dress up the dead body," this way or that, while leaving it still lifeless and void of God's active presence, then just how fruitful are they?

Everything that flows from heaven gives life, and every emphasis of Scripture, *when* under the influence of Holy Spirit, will quicken, revive, and bring life, as it is the *living* Word of God. "The first MAN, Adam, became a living soul. The last Adam (Jesus) *became* a life-giving spirit*." 1Corinthians 15:45 NASB.

The very last thing Satan wants is the body of Christ to recognize its lifeless, spiritual bankruptcy, and unitedly agree that we will cease all other prioritized activity for the sake of the most vital priority – His presence and power. It is no coincidence that the main theme of the entire New Testament is the death of Jesus and the resurrecting empowering of the Holy Spirit, restored into man once again.

Such a shift of focus in our lives and as a whole, would truly display Jesus "on earth as it is in Heaven." Ephesians 2:13-22 elaborates on how the cross of Christ disintegrated the manmade cultural and religious boundaries that had separated the Jew and Gentile, and through *one* Holy Spirit, united all believers as *one new man* unto our Father.

In the natural, it isn't hard to function in a particular country or work environment where each person is allowed to segregate themselves into like-minded people, whether it be their ethnicity, religious views, or social preferences. But what has always been a clear sign of heaven's culture superseding our own prejudices, is when a diverse group of people have become united through the Holy Spirit and are functioning effectively well together. The culture of heaven has become their new lifestyle, and therefore, a testimony to the onlooking world that only something or someone supernatural could cause such a strong unity with "those ingredients." This very kind of unity was demonstrated in the early church:

> [41] So then, those who had received his word were baptized; and that day there were added about three thousand souls. [42] They were *continually* devoting themselves to the apostles' teaching and to fellowship, to the breaking of bread and to prayer.[43] Everyone kept feeling a *sense of awe*; and _many wonders and_ signs were taking place through the apostles. [44] And all those who had believed were together and had all things in common; [45] and they *began* selling their property and possessions and were sharing them with all, as anyone might have need. [46] Day by day continuing with one mind in the temple, and breaking bread from house to house, they were taking their meals together with gladness and sincerity of heart,[47] praising God and having favor with all the people. And the Lord was adding to their number day by day those who were being saved. -Acts 2:41-47 NASB.
>
> This is immediately following Peter's first sermon (after His baptism of the Holy Spirit) where 3,000 people from all over the world had come, listened, and believed. They were now united as one new man/body with only the Holy Spirit getting the credit for such a supernatural atmosphere of heaven on earth. I love how it said, "Everyone (and that means everyone) kept feeling a sense of awe, and many (not occasional) signs and wonders were taking place."

Where has this sense of awe gone? Has Jesus and the Holy Spirit become boring? Has He taken a leave of absence from the supernatural signs and wonders that were clearly evident in the early church? That's what religion will tell us, in order to try and make sense of the clear symptoms of a dead, lifeless, powerless body. But you and I can wake up from our body's true condition, first as individuals, then corporately together, and believe in God's way of unity, endorsement, and ministry – the supernatural presence and power of the Holy Spirit.

Everything Jesus commissioned us to (commission=co-laboring with Jesus' supernatural ministry) is completely *impossible* apart from the tangible presence of Holy Spirit. "Heal the sick, raise the dead, cast out demons..." is what He tells us in Mark 16.

> *It's the ministry of Jesus continued through His Spirit*
> *that restores the "awe and wonder" of God back into*
> *His people and into the earth once again.*

When a people resign their own manmade titles, ambitions, pride, and egos and fix their eyes on Him, refusing to go forward apart from the tangible presence and power of God, the Lord will not merely visit them, but inhabit there and, as a result, He, Himself will "add to their number daily." (Acts 2:47). The Lord does all the hard stuff if we'd stop trying to do it for Him. Do you believe His presence is enough? Do you believe Jesus is qualified enough to be the actual leader of your church? Do you believe the *head* has the power and ability to direct the *body*? Regardless of what we say, our theology, our actions, and lack of fruit have shown the answer is *no*. We have exchanged truth for the numerous lies of the enemy and it has caused a dismembered body just flapping to and fro, while we confidently believe we are fine as long as we keep telling ourselves that.

But *how* can we become a people once again possessed by the Spirit of the living God? A people, where the surrounding community knows that we don't merely meet with one another once a week to do the *church thing*, but we meet with the very tangible, liberating, miraculous, presence of the living God. A people that no longer carry on with our manmade productions/programs where we refer to Him in such religious abstract ways, as if He's not actually there in the room with us.

It starts with you and me. To be a church, centered and possessed by the tangible presence, power, love, and voice of God, we first must be an individual that will allow Him to have such Lordship over us. An individual, hungering for more of God's tangible presence, regardless of how your pastor, Mom/Dad, spouse, sibling, co-worker, neighbor, Bible study group feels about it. Nobody else's influence is as important as our personal decision to venture into the *more* of God.

Please understand when I say, "more of God" I don't mean He has been holding Himself back or is waiting for us to meet a condition before He gives more of Himself. Jesus' death has already qualified every believer to currently have "all spiritual blessings in Christ," Eph. 1:3. But I'm referring to our minds being renewed to New Covenant truth, so that our spiritual awareness and sensitivity are tuned in to what He's already given us, so that we can *experience* the fullness of His presence more than what we currently are.

Sometimes we have to reach the point of exhaustion from our own methods, efforts, and ideas to finally be open to what God has been trying to get us to walk into the whole time. As I began to hunger after the practical ways of God, His tangible presence and fruit, etc., He brought me to what has been most pivotal in my walk with God – the key to "reviving the lifeless body" with His Spirit once again:

THE SECRET PLACE

I'll explain what I mean by this subtitle as we continue. The religious lifestyle is one where our identity has become wrapped up in what we doctrinally/theologically believe, or not, while minimal practical experiencing of God's presence/power is actually engaged. Therefore, you rarely hear any discussion or assessment in such circles of how much *practical time* is spent in our day/week/life with His presence.

It's as if that *practical time* in His presence is a bonus or just a good thing to help supplement your spiritual life rather than the very source vital to living. When I began to inquire from God as to why His supernatural tangible presence/power wasn't in me or my church, but instead, in these other various ministries, He began to show me that at their roots was a greater intimacy of quality time spent in His presence than what I'd experienced. The supernatural fruit coming out of their lives was simply an overflow of constant communion with the Holy Spirit. As He began to show me this, I quickly felt my religious ego challenged, as I realized how immature I was with this presence-centered lifestyle idea.

The reality was, I wasn't used to truly being engaged with God's presence while at work, pumping gas, grocery shopping, and hanging out with friends. I guess I didn't believe He'd want to talk to me so practically and frequently in the midst of such trivial errands and tasks. It's because I just didn't believe, practically speaking, that He wanted me to step into such a practical walking with Him that was fueled by His tangible presence and present tense voice speaking to me. So, I needed to be recalibrated to say the least. My expectancy levels needed a quantum upgrade. And the first "charging station" if you will, would be in the **secret place** with God.

There's only one way to hear what the Father is saying and do only what He is doing. It isn't a formula, doctrine, or recital of certain phrases... it isn't a certain prayer to repeat every morning. Becoming the very voice and expression of heavenly Father cannot be watered down to such man-made theories or theology. Instead, Jesus' example says it all:

> [12] Now it came to pass in those days that He went out to the mountain to pray, and continued all night in prayer to God. Luke 6:12 NKJV.

> [23] And when He had sent the multitudes away, He went up on the mountain by Himself to pray. Now when evening came, He was alone there. Matthew 14:23 NKJV.

"Pray," in the original language, isn't as many of us think of it today: Just spouting off our wish list to God and asking for forgiveness, etc. Instead, when Jesus went all night to pray, it actually means to "interact with, exchange ideas (converse, a two-way conversation, not one way)" with the Father. When we actually change the way we're approaching Him to the way Jesus did, we'll find His presence becoming more evident and tangible to us, as we will be positioned to receive from Him as our heavenly Father, the way He has always intended. What's amazing to me, is that, despite all the amazing miracles, signs and wonders, and profound sermons Jesus shared, the disciples recognized there was a root to all of this "supernatural fruit" and they asked Him to better understand it: "Now it came to pass, as He was praying in a certain place, when He ceased, *that* one of His disciples said to Him, "Lord, teach us to pray, as John also taught his disciples." Luke 11:1 NKJV. It is here Jesus teaches them the Lord's prayer. In Matthew's Gospel, he adds some very important things Jesus said before going into the famously quoted prayer:

> "When you pray, you are not to be like the hypocrites; for they love to stand and pray in the synagogues and on the street corners so that they may be seen by men. Truly I say to you, they have their reward in full. [6] But you, when you pray, *go into your **inner room** ("closet"-KJV), close your door and pray to your Father who is in **secret**, and your Father who sees what is done in secret will reward you*[7] "And when you are praying, do not use meaningless repetition as the Gentiles do, for they suppose that they will be heard for their many words. [8] So do not be like them; for your Father knows what you need before you ask Him.[9] "Pray, then, in this way: 'Our Father who is in heaven, Hallowed be Your name...'" –Matthew 6:5-9 NASB.

Do you currently take what Jesus says as literal? I know I didn't for a very long time. I never made a "secret place" designed just so the Lord and I could talk to one another. The truth is I didn't truly believe that kind of intimacy was available and desired from Him. I didn't realize He wanted to use what He once said and did from Scripture to teach me how to hear and see what He is presently doing and saying to me and those around me today. I didn't even treat Him or think of Him in this way.

It was kind of weird to me, and I was just so used to doing my devotional and going about my day, then going to church once a week. It's easy to fall into whatever popular, religiously correct external behavioral trends are around and receive the approval of our fellow church members, leaders, and pastors. We can believe this religious activity means we're spiritual, while yet be far from God. But Jesus is describing in this verse what living for the audience of one (God) is all about.

Like I briefly mentioned last chapter, I'd started to come to the sad realization of how small an amount of time I was actually spent with God per day and per week. I remember thinking, "Hmm, I actually spend more time watching a secular movie on a Saturday night than all the time I spend with God during the week, combined." Yet, what was even more sad, is how normal this was to me and my fellow church members, pastors, and even conference officials. Could it be that the obvious lack of supernatural presence and works of God in our congregation and lives was in direct correlation to how little we valued His tangible presence and voice in our own lives the other six days of the week? Could it be we had exchanged intimacy with Jesus for a false sense of religious security in the theology and doctrines we believed to be so superior to other, fellow Christians? Unfortunately, I found this to be true, not only in myself, but among many other denominational groups. We can be so quick to clarify what type of Christian we are by the name of the denomination we are a part of. But Biblically speaking, the true Christian, is the one where the presence of Christ dwells in, speaks through, and possesses.

If you haven't done so yet, I'd encourage you to dedicate a room, closet, or space in your home to create your secret place. This is where intimate, real time with Jesus can be experienced each morning, night, or whenever you want to just be with Him away from distractions. It's not that you can't engage His presence wherever or whenever, but it's similar to how a husband and wife dedicate their bedroom for their private talks and time together, behind closed doors, away from distractions, and away from the noise. Some have referred to it as a "war room," but in reality, our "warring" is effortlessly effective when our gaze is fixed on the bliss of His presence.

I had to ask myself, "What would be something I've never given God the opportunity for in my life before?" I had reached the point of being tired of where my efforts and powerless theology had taken me when compared to the early church/disciples of Jesus, but would I truly venture to surrender in a way I had yet to up to this point? Several scriptures reveal such an exploration into the secrets of God is something He longs for us to personally discover:

"You will seek Me and find *Me* when you search for
Me with all your heart. Jeremiah 29:13 NASB.

"The secret of the LORD IS FOR THOSE WHO FEAR HIM,
And He will make them know His covenant." Psalm
25:14 NASB.

"It is the glory of God to conceal a matter,
But the glory of kings is to search out a matter."
Proverbs 25:2 NASB.

And these texts are from the Old Covenant era so imagine how much more superior of a connection and reality we now can experience when devoting more of our time to Him?

You've probably heard the saying, "if you want to go where you haven't gone you have to be willing to do what you've never done." So, I prayed, and I felt convicted to start spending about an hour-plus each morning. This was a block of time set apart to allow His Spirit to lead, guide, and reveal Himself to me. But, the more of His presence I experienced, the hungrier He made me for more.

In the natural realm, we get fuller the more food we eat, but I've found in the spiritual realm the more we eat (spend time in His presence) the hungrier it makes you for even more. That's why, at first, dedicating such time may seem like a spiritual discipline but it quickly turns into an incredible, effortless delight. I thought, "If I'm enjoying this degree of His presence with one hour, what would happen if I could spend even more time with Him?" So, then I felt impressed to dedicate three to five hours a morning with Him, from 3:00 am to 8:00 am. (Please note these times, etc. are not formulas, nor being presented as such, but instead I encourage you to pray and follow whatever you get impressed with from God). "What would I do for three-plus hours?" I thought. "Well, I guess all I could do is ask for Holy Spirit to guide me into whatever I needed to do that morning to be engaged with His presence and voice."

And that started the most precious time of my day/life-intimacy with Jesus. Having no formula or method to follow was so contrary to what I was used to. We often find comfort in formulas and theories because it's predictable and therefore we equate predictability with safe. But regarding the things of God, "without faith it is impossible to please Him..." (Heb.11:6), therefore, His ways are typically opposite of such man-made securities and rely on His present tense leading. Remember man is to live by "every word that *proceeds* from the mouth of God (present tense)" not "that once proceeded," past tense). In fact, that word *proceeds,* in the original language means "every word that continually keeps coming." Hence, why He led me to just entrusting the agenda for the three hours to whatever the Holy Spirit impressed me to each new morning.

I remember struggling to let the Holy Spirit lead with this, as I was so programed to be "doing" all the time and placed certain value on doing certain things over others, such as reading the Bible, over listening and worshiping. But I've been learning firsthand how He loves to spontaneously lead us, and the moment we are beginning to box Him into a formula, He quickly leads us into something else to shake it off of us and position us with childlike dependency and expectancy for where He is leading next. So, as crazy as this may sound to some, these three to five hours would fly right by.

My agenda was resigned to His and posturing myself before His presence like this allowed my body, soul, and spirit to recognize and prioritize the Lordship and leading of God's tangible presence above all other previous methods. You can say one thing acknowledging something in theory and yet practically be unchanged, but this was a *practical submission* which, in turn, yielded practical change. He led me to Scripture, worship, to remain still to hear what thoughts He was putting in my heart, versus my own, watching sermons and testimonies, writing, praying, interceding, soaking in worship music while contemplating His goodness and ways. A lot of times He'd highlight an area that I was most inquisitive about in my heart and have me search the Scriptures or other inspired teachings on that topic. For example, coming from a very religious background, I realized I had difficulty truly believing my redeemed identity as a son, versus the religious slave like in the Old Covenant perspective (a very common challenge in many religious circles). One of the resources He led me to regarding this topic were YouTube videos from a pastor named Dan Mohler. I heard Pastor Dan teach and preach the Gospel in such provoking ways that upheld a standard of love so much higher than what I'd known or heard. One of the series he did is called, *Power and Love.* They were very helpful to me with this topic. It made my heart burn for a deeper transformation of pure love for God and others.

The one goal from these three-plus hours had to be clear: engaging with God's presence Himself. Not merely read *about* God. Not, *do* for God. Simply and practically, engage with Him, one on one, personally, intimately, transparently, and submissively vulnerable to Him unlike ever before.

Even while I was listening to a teaching or sermon I was conversing with God as I would a friend during a movie. The results? Life changing, a heavenly provoking to experience more, an overwhelming satisfaction, unspeakable joy, peace and yet a hungering for God that just gets deeper and all consuming.

The time that it would normally take for my own thoughts, worries, and anxieties to cease and rest in His presence began to happen quicker and quicker. It became easier to sense His tangible presence with me and to hear His voice speaking to my heart over my own. Not only that, but then throughout the day it was much easier to remain engaged with His presence and to reengage if I became distracted with something. At first, I remember thinking, "Wow He's talking to me so much more now." But soon, I realized He had always been talking to me, I just didn't recognize the sound of His voice and the ways He was speaking to me. Unlike a memory verse or religious doctrine that can be easily memorized in our head and regurgitated, His voice and ways are only experienced from intimate time in His presence. It's in His presence that you will realize His affections and love for you are as specific, full, and complete as if there was no other human on earth to share them with. In reality, there is only one *you*. So, the experience you have with Him is unmatched to anybody else's. This is why He longs for us to give Him this sacred time. He died for you and Him to never again have to be without it.

Regardless of where a person is or isn't in their relationship with God, His intention, desires, and plans for us have never changed. You and I have been created and designed to live for this very moment for a specific destiny that only His present leading and voice alone can empower us to live out in this earth for eternal results. That's why the devil is trying so hard to hinder us from such a practical experiencing of God.

> 27 "The sheep that are My own *hear My voice and listen to Me*; I know them, and they follow Me." -John 10:27 AMP.

A pastor named Bill Johnson once said, "Jesus didn't say 'My sheep know my book,' but 'My sheep know My voice.'" The only hope of walking out our God given, gigantic destinies, is close, practical, proximity to our Good Shepherd Jesus. It's in this secret place He shares the secrets of His heart for your life. Apart from His present speaking, leading, and activity in our lives, we are sure to be easy prey for the wolf, Satan. But entrusting ourselves to Him, we are surely protected by His rod and led by His staff, "Thy rod and thy staff comfort me..." –Psalms 23:4.

While learning the various ways God speaks, we can become vulnerable in our childlike excitement. With Holy Spirit's leading this is perfectly okay and, in fact, necessary to yield to a greater heart transformation. However, know that His "secrets" for you would never violate His nature or sacred principles of Scripture. Instead, His voice and the fresh revelations He shares with you will build on His Word and take you deeper into His pure truths in ways that will bring you into greater, practical, personal applications of these truths.

A biblical Christian is defined and *endorsed by heaven* by the actual life of Jesus reduplicated in us through the ongoing experiencing of Holy Spirit communion permeating our everything more and more each day.

> "18 And we all, with unveiled face, *continually* seeing as in a mirror the glory of the Lord, are *progressively* being transformed into His image from [one degree of] glory to [even more] glory, *which comes from the Lord, [who is] the Spirit.*" 2 Corinthians 3:18 AMP.

There it is. Did you catch that? Look at all the present tense experiential words used there describing this. Notice *how* we are transformed into Jesus image: First, "By *continually* seeing as in a mirror the glory of the Lord" therefore "are progressively being transformed into His image from one degree of glory to even more glory," and this all happens by a constant inflow and experiencing of the Spirit, who comes from the Lord. Presence, presence, presence. You and I currently reflect the image and person of Jesus to the degree we are "continually seeing the glory of the Lord." Which means five to ten minutes a day will only produce the degree of His image and presence that correlates to that, which pales compared to the example of Jesus and the early church.

Religiosity emphasizes reflecting Jesus image is based on the accuracy of doctrine we believe/teach, hence, why the denominational name is stressed with pride despite the clear lack of heaven's endorsement (i.e., supernatural power, presence, signs/wonders Jesus said should follow believers).

Following Jesus is aligning ourselves with the *priorities* of Jesus who is THE way, THE truth, and THE life and is what we should set our hearts and lives on. THEN and only then will everything else naturally follow in with the *proper importance and weight* placed on it as the heaven would have it. *So many people are trying to decipher doctrine and interpretation of the scriptures without the intimate presence of the Lord from whom the scriptures were written from, and they claim to have "the truth."*

Once again, look at the last time man approached God in such a shallow way in the Old Covenant: instructions and doctrine were written down, told to a people, and they supposedly followed the instructions, while neglecting actual communion and relationship with the God who had given it to them. *When His presence isn't prioritized as THE MOST important aspect of our spirituality, it's impossible to accurately decipher His voice, written Word, and more, despite what popular religion may say and practice.* Man has come up with so many countless endorsements to label one as "learned" or "educated in the scriptures," which has left many with a false sense of security, and lack of actual spiritual depth according to heaven's assessment. We've come up with seminaries, Bible schools, colleges, church titles, and others to create levels of spiritual endorsement that only we have placed manmade honor on. Please understand I'm not against theological formal education or training, but rather the mis-prioritization of them in light of the priorities Jesus modeled as most important. The sad part is that it's very common for people to be fooled by such manmade endorsements. Under their "human glory," they quote a scripture and give their own interpretation of it while having absolutely no divine endorsement, because it didn't actually come from His presence and intimacy with Him.

> *Declaring the "Word of the Lord" has surprisingly very little to do with the mere memorization of scripture, doctrine, hermeneutics, etc. It has everything to do with the actual Lord Himself and the proximity to Him we practically live from; the time we spend living in and from His presence.* His written Word was always intended to lead us into such practical, real intimacy with Him today, and never as an exchange for it.

I've found that He loves to bring us into the awe and wonder of who He is. Once I started to see more of heaven's practical side in tangible ways, I began to keep a *Glory Journal* of supernatural signs and wonders, dreams, visions, angelic activity, and much more. It may sound crazy to some, but what's humbled me the most is how much He had always been speaking but I just hadn't been able to recognize His voice and ways, because I truly didn't believe it was even possible for us today.

Does that resonate with you perhaps? I used to think that for someone to have such things taking place must mean they are either superior in their spiritual life to the majority of people around or I would be extremely skeptical to even believe it was from God, but rather the devil. But I pray you soon understand and actually grow to believe this: Jesus' death is what has made us ALL worthy of such intimacy with our Heavenly Father, Savior, and Holy Spirit. I pray right now that Holy Spirit come and stir inside of you a deep hunger for a more practical relationship with God than ever before. I invite you to pray this prayer out loud:

> Jesus, I pray any degree of religiosity that has caused me to have layers of unbelief in my heart, to disintegrate as Holy Spirit and the ongoing revelation of Himself continues to penetrate beyond them and usher me into your presence even now Jesus. I command my Heart to be open. Ears be open. Eyes be open. Mind be open. In Jesus' name.

I promise, if you truly posture yourself in an attitude of receiving directly from the Lord, not from me, He is sure to use what's in this book beyond your intellect and into a greater personal, spiritual walk with Him unlike anything you've experienced so far.

If you feel like you're at a spiritual plateau right now, needing further insight, direction, or acceleration with "what's next" for you in your life, I promise, if you dare to take this invitation from Jesus as a first priority *above all else* up to this point, a practical surrendering to "seeking first the Kingdom of God and His righteousness" then "all these things" and so much more, will surely be added to you. (Mat. 6:33).

I've personally seen and experienced that every man or woman, boy or girl, ministry, church, or pastor that is *currently* walking out authentic *supernatural* signs, wonders, and miracles for the kingdom of heaven, has *first* come to the sobering reality of their bankruptcy without a *lifestyle*, who's priority is a ceaseless engaging with the tangible presence and voice of God – namely intimacy with Jesus.

> *There are no shortcuts, formulas, or special phrases*
> *to merely regurgitate while being apart from prac-*
> *tical intimacy with Jesus.*

When religious people come to that reality, which is completely contrary to the formula filled religions of today, they either surrender to Him with a fuller "yes" or look for ways to discredit such ministries, in order to protect their religious ego from the obvious lacking of supernatural fruit in their own lives and ministry.

I have seen that many of the religious skeptics and critics of the supernatural, are individuals who greatly lacked in this area (the secret place) and were just looking for ways to label what they were actually challenged by from these ministries. You will find, more often than not, religious persecution is always nearby the genuine moving of God's signs, wonders, and manifestations. You'll find the YouTube videos, sermons, and even ministries who feel their "call" is to expose the deceptions of such things, yet they, themselves lack the endorsement of heaven of supernatural signs, wonders, and the tangible presence of God.

In fact, the Lord showed me numerous times in dreams, of the religious persecution arising against what He is building in and through us, and the ways we are and will be labeled by the skeptical, doubtful religious community. He warned His disciples, (the ones in *closest* proximity to Him, the ones hearing His present-tense voice, and following Him, despite the religious persecution), "If they persecuted me, they will persecute you..." John 15:20.

There is always an arrogant spirit behind religious persecution and always a clear lack of the tangible presence and power of God, which indicates how much God isn't the source of what they are saying and doing in their slandering of the body. 2 Timothy 3:5 warns us of this very thing "in the last days" there will be those who have a *"form* of godliness (modern religion/religiosity) while denying the *power* thereof (God's power)."

When the bad news (the deceptions and lies we must warn others about) becomes more interesting and fascinating to focus on and share, then we are missing the point of how *good* the Good News really is. When we are experiencing a vibrant, growing relationship with the Living Christ, He becomes the all-consuming fire that saturates our thoughts, our actions, affections and floods our entire being to be the springs of living water that others can drink from (Jn 4:14).

I've learned, before judging other ministries, manifestations of the Spirit, ways people express themselves through worship and prayer (a challenge for me, especially coming from my particular religious background), was to realize they could have a much more mature intimate or secret place than exists in my life and, therefore, bear different fruit than I have. They could have a more mature spiritual life, than mine and, therefore, be more sensitive to His presence than I currently am.

So, what do I do? I hang up my preconceived judgments, ideas, and prejudices and simply entrust myself more to Him, believing Him to be God and bound by no human reasoning's or methodology. I invite you to do the same, as your exploration of the kingdom of heaven continues to unfold into the divine exploits and adventures you were created for. No need to police those things that God is *more than capable* of keeping in check. I promise if we fix our eyes, and I mean fix with an unwavering gaze, "onto Jesus, the author and finisher of our faith," (Heb.12:2), He will not lead us astray.

> "And [knowing that they listen] He calls his own sheep
> by name and leads them out [to pasture]. ⁴When He
> has brought all his own *sheep* outside, He walks on

ahead of them, and the sheep follow him because *they know His voice and recognize his call.*[5] They will never follow a stranger, but will run away from him, because they do not know the voice of strangers."
John 10:3-5

I believe God wants to stir in you a greater desire to hear His voice and to sense His tangible presence beyond what you have experienced up to this point.

In our next chapter, we'll dive into some of my personal encounters and experiences, which I pray will be provoking to you, in a positive manner. I believe right now you have a personal invitation from Jesus Himself, to be led into a greater engagement with Holy Spirit in the secret place, one that will blow you away with a greater reality of the living God unlike ever before. Pray this prayer out loud with me:

Jesus, I want to hear your voice and the secrets of Your heart for my life. I want You to eradicate from my heart any lie or deception I've embraced in exchange for this reality. I want to truly, practically, know and experience Your voice and have a hunger in my life to not move a foot forward without hearing it. Make the distinguishing difference of Your written Word and Your tangible voice clearer to me so that I don't abuse one to cover the lack of the other. In Jesus' name, Amen.

CHAPTER 6

GOD SPEAKS IN ANGELIC ACTIVITY

"How can our son grow up without a father figure in his life and learn how to be a man?" A worried mother said.

Her husband answered her. "Look, everything will be fine. I'm going to write him several letters that will tell him how much I have always loved him."

The husband figured the matter settled and left the room, closing the door a bit too forcefully. His wife stood, tears streaming down her face. He'd left his child – never to return. As the child grew, the mother saw an empty void in the face of her son. She knew her son sought the affirmation, guidance, love, and embrace of his own father.

Out of desperation to try and comfort her son, at each birthday, first day of school, accomplishment, and significant life event, the mother would go and grab the letters his father had pre-written and give them to her son. The boy would read them and re-read them. Then, with eyes closed, he imagined his father being physically present and speaking those very words to him, only to open his eyes and realize it was just his imagination. His father wasn't there with him.

Over time, as the boy got older, he had memorized the words of his father, and yet lacked so many practical life lessons that could only come through a father participating in the boy's life. This became evident to him more and more as he couldn't help but notice the undeveloped areas in his life, compared to his friends whose fathers were present. The deep wound continued to expand, and whenever he would hear the word father from his friends, he would cringe, because he could only define the meaning as a distant person who'd once written letters and once expressed his love to him, while abandoning him. The thought of going somewhere with his father, enjoying a game with him, or just being hugged by him, was completely foreign and the very thought seemed too good to be true and, even selfish, to imagine it as a necessity.

In today's society of physiological study, we would say the child in the example above would need years of counseling, guidance, and mentorship to cope with such an absence of his father. We'd quickly identify so many undeveloped areas, emotionally, physically, and mentally as a result of having no father present during each critical phase of life. The difference of a physically-present father would allow the father to actually guide his son through the many new challenges he'd face.

We see, in the natural world, how vital it is to grow up with the present tense involvement, care, guidance, love, and joy that comes from a father son/daughter relationship. Yet the biggest deception I see in the church today, is portraying our heavenly Father in the exact same distant way portrayed in this parable.

But His written Word, the Bible (His letters), were never meant to replace His tangible presence and voice, specific and unique to what is presently happening in each moment of our lives.

Many lies of the devil have become so popularly embraced, that so many of God's children live as if they are mere orphans, hoping to one day be adopted in the future. Just as we see in the natural example, so it is in the spiritual – if a child doesn't have their needs/desires fulfilled from their present heavenly Father, that child will then be in a constant search to have his/her needs met from another source. It's easy to look at a body of believers in a church and say, "Look at all the hypocrisy, gossip, and backbiting. Such immaturity." However, with that thought, we might not see beyond those things to their root, which is children searching to be loved, validated, accepted, approved, and appraised in a way that only their heavenly Father can fulfill. He longs to personally express all that and more, to each of us.

When the true, pure Gospel is taught and our redeemed identities embraced, immature fruit quickly disappear. I've seen firsthand this very transformation in our own personal lives and in the lives of many bodies of believers. It is truly powerful testament to the living God. Typical barriers of race, prejudice, selfishness, and class disintegrate when the orphan spirit is replaced with the wholesome identity of a son or daughter of the living God.

Many religious circles believe that miracles, signs, and wonders stopped when the Bible was completed. They'll say, "There's no need for such things because they are the lesser things God gave until the greater written Word would be given." In many of these circles, to desire anything more than the written Word of God is viewed as selfish, unbelieving, and even weak.

I recently heard one popular religious leader say that, "Signs, wonders, and miracles are for the baby Christian and we should mature to relying only on the written Word of God alone." The thing with deception is that it comes with some truth mixed in with the lies. Should we rely on the written Word of God? Absolutely. But are signs, wonders, and miracles only for baby Christians? If so, then Peter, Paul, and Jesus, Himself, would all be considered baby Christians with such a standard, and we know they obviously weren't. Jesus was the perfect example of how a mature son of God should live. He was constantly operating in supernatural signs and wonders. Numerous times in Scripture, angels attended to Him. Yet, He didn't discard the written Word of God, but often quoted it to affirm and elaborate on its realities for the present time He was in.

It's no coincidence that such ministries and people who believe such a deception about signs and wonders lack the tangible presence and power of God. This was true for me, for the majority of my life. Sometimes we can feel the need to create such false doctrine to explain the clear lack of the Holy Spirit's presence and fruit. Just like the Pharisees, I had learned to explain away any concern for the lack of such practical supernatural fruit, by believing it was my "superior spiritual maturity of biblical understanding and doctrine that truly mattered."

However, nowhere in scripture does it say there's an expiration date for signs, wonders, and miracles. Instead I've found that only false doctrine aims at destroying the present voice, the tangible presence, and experiencing of the living God for today.

Satan fears for you and me to actually believe the reality of the Gospel and power of the living Christ, because we'd become dispensers of the same genuine, living Jesus, instead of mere reciters of what God once said and once did. Again, scripture warns of "A form of godliness denying the power thereof..." in 2 Timothy 3:5, which I've found to be the root of the spirit of religiosity, which is truly demonic in nature, as it cripples God's people from walking out our God-given power.

When I first started to experience the tangible presence and voice of God, I grew a disgust for the many lies I'd believed from the enemy. As a result, I remember getting frustrated when I'd hear others around me express with pride their belief in those same lies.

I'd say to the Lord, "God if they only knew you are so much more real than that." But, over time the Lord began to show me that's just it. Behind all of those skeptical, unbelieving, doubting theologies and explanations, is an unbelief in the living God, who can and will express Himself beyond the written Word. Truly, it's an unbelief that He is actually a good Father.

We settle for the deadbeat dad in the parable, who abandons His child or perhaps our own negative experience with our earthly father.

But His written Word is actually a compilation of practical encounters normal men and women experienced with the super-natural God. It shouldn't be such a shock that He's still the same today. We love to quote, "He's the same yesterday, today, and for-ever," for other examples – but why not for this? When it comes to the supernatural parts of the Bible, we develop selective hearing and application instead of seeing the whole Bible as the supernat-ural standard we grow up into. We can either find out why, how, and where He's still supernatural today or create some explanation to defend why He isn't.

As my spiritual hunger grew, God began to lead me to more gen-uine believers who showed His supernatural fruit marking their lives. However, I also found that near every authentic resource, ministry or church, held some religious skeptic, anti-supernatural religious ministry, or pastor trying to expose the error of the authentic. They'd try to give a rationalization as to why the miracles and manifesta-tions had to be demonic and not from God. With my own past of religious skepticisms these explanations would begin to cause me to fear once again. But then, God would remind me, "It's important to follow Jesus' way of prioritizing our focus, according to heaven and not man's hypothesis," so that we're not led back into the paralyzing spirit of religiosity again.

He'd invite me to share my fears and concerns with Him during our time together in the morning and invite His Spirit to give me pure revelation with all I was trying to process. He showed me that when a person or ministry's time, energies, and focus has shifted to one of warning everyone about other ministries, pastors, or teachings they've supposedly exposed, more than likely they've lost sight of any good news, good enough to captivate people's attention. Which is why they feel the need to discuss and warn people about the bad news. They might think they are doing their duty to protect their listeners, but at the root is a lack of trust in the Holy Spirit's abilities to lead/guide, versus the devil's ability to deceive. But the authentic good news of the Gospel will hold your attention captive unlike anything this world could ever offer you in exchange.

So much of the struggle the church has in having a single eye unto the Lord is because they've settled for something other than the practical truth we're talking about. It's easy to get distracted with secular media, movies, and much more, when we're taught to believe in such a distant Father, and are told just to recite those letters (memory verses) when we're feeling the urge to forget about Him for a moment of fleshly pleasure. But I've experienced first-hand how effortlessly our devotion, surrender, and love for Him flows from deep within us, when we are learning how to hear His present voice and experience His present presence.

For most of my life, I had in my heart and practical belief a BIG picture of the devil and a small picture of God. (Notice I said in my "practical belief" because theologically, I would have told you differently.) This is because we'll recognize all the present-tense ways Satan speaks and encounters us while ignoring all of God's present-tense ways, believing Him to be limited to His written Word. It is imperative we start inclining and engaging every part of our being to the present-tense voice and presence of our heavenly Father because He is intently interested in everything we do and wants to engage us to experiencing His love beyond His love letters. We get it, when it comes to father and son, husband and wife, yet we've somehow settled for such dysfunctional lies about the God who created us to never be apart from His presence.

ANGELIC ACTIVITY CARRYING THE PRESENT "WORD OF THE LORD"

In Scripture, there is an abundance of records of experiences with God's tangible voice and ways. If we allow, these stories can provoke us to believe in His desire to express Himself through the same and even greater, tangible ways to us today. Since one of the most anti-presence theologies says that God only did such supernatural things because they didn't have Scripture yet, I want to highlight just a few of many examples to the contrary:

> [26] Now in the sixth month the angel Gabriel was sent from God to a city in Galilee called Nazareth, [27] to a virgin engaged to a man whose name was Joseph, of the descendants of David; and the virgin's name was Mary. [28] And coming in, he said to her, "Greetings, favored one. The Lord *is* with you." [29] But she was very perplexed at *this* statement, and kept pondering what kind of salutation this was. [30] The angel said to her, "Do not be afraid, Mary; for you have found favor with God. [31] And behold, you will conceive in your womb and bear a son, and you shall name Him Jesus. [32] He will be great and will be called the Son of the Most High; and the Lord God will give Him the throne of His father David; [33] and He will reign over the house of Jacob forever, and His kingdom will have no end." [34] Mary said to the angel, "How can this be, since I am a virgin?" [35] The angel answered and said to her, "The Holy Spirit will come upon you, and the power of the Most High will overshadow you; and for that reason the holy Child shall be called the Son of God. [36] And behold, even your relative Elizabeth has also conceived a son in her old age; and she who was called barren is now in her sixth month. [37] For nothing will be impossible with God." [38] And Mary said, "Behold, the bondslave of the Lord; may it be done to me according to your word." And the angel departed from her." Luke 1:26-38 NASB.

Isaiah 7:14 had prophesied of the messiah being born of a virgin, and this book was very popular at this time, along with other books of the Old Testament. Despite it being foretold in God's written Word, He delivered a personalized message to Mary declaring what God's written Word had already foretold, but now was a practical reality for her. Not only that, but He even explained how this would happen to her – which, in many religious circles today, her inquiry for the practical question of "how" would be viewed as immature. Notice by the end of this encounter with the angel, Gabriel, she received this as directly from the Lord and declared "May it be done to me according to Your word." His word to her brought her into a present tense embrace of God's Word. Notice the angel didn't contradict God's Word, but simply led her to a personal embracing of it in the present reality through this supernatural encounter. God is the same today. His present tense voice, presence, and supernatural encounters never contradict His written Word, but simply bring us into a *personal/practical* experience today. Gabriel also elaborated into more specific details that would help Mary gain a clearer understanding of what the Lord was doing, while still not contradicting the written prophecy. The written Word wasn't a ceiling, but instead a framework the angel could elaborate on, based on what the Lord wanted him to share with her. The intimacies we are invited to experience with Jesus are personal, not general, and the more we learn to hear, see, and believe in God's *present activity*, the more our beliefs and lives will align with the living God of today.

Angels are mentioned over 270 times in the Bible and frequently throughout Scripture to deliver personalized revelation, messages, and warnings. Hebrews 1:14 says, [14]"Are they not all ministering spirits, sent out to render service for the sake of those who will inherit salvation?" The reality is, I truly didn't believe they were still *on duty* for us today *in the same practical ways described in scripture*. Yet, from Genesis to Revelation, there are countless encounters between humans and these precious messengers of God. In fact, if this seems to be stretching you, (as far as believing they are still interested in ministering to you today), I invite you to search out how often God uses them throughout the scriptures both Old and New Testament. Some people believe they were only necessary in the Old Testament. However, the cross has allowed us to more in synch with heaven's ways than ever before in history.

We often will say things like, "Man, I wish I could have been alive back then to have such encounters." But they actually were the ones who longed to see and experience our day, as the boundaries sin had caused *would be removed* and we'd no longer have to be separate from God's presence, thanks to the victory of the cross. [17] "For truly I say to you that many prophets and righteous men desired to see what you see, and did not see *it*, and to hear what you hear, and did not hear *it*." – Matthew 13:17.

The reality is, the New Testament believers had so embraced the finished work of the cross that signs, wonders, and angelic activity had become the norm of the Christians. "[12] At the hands of the apostles *many* signs and wonders were taking place among the people;" Acts 5:12. Key word, "many" not just "on a special occasion." The activity of angels manifesting and co-laboring was so common to the early church, that when Peter came to the house of some believers (after an angel had supernaturally led him out of his prison cell), the girl told them "Peter is at the gate." However, they kept telling her, "You're out of your mind... it's his angel." (Acts 12:15) If you or I knew an Angel was standing outside of our door, would we not rush over to open it? But when we are co-laboring with heaven as God has always intended us to, the encounters and interactions with the supernatural becomes our *new normal* as it is the natural birthright of redeemed sons and daughters of God. Jesus was the first example of how a redeemed son would operate with the supernatural (not the last) and, in the desert described in Matthew chapter 4, and also in the garden of Gethsemane, it is recorded, "Angels came and ministered to Him."

Our present lack of effectiveness in the earth isn't due to heaven not providing us with the proper equipping for the work at hand, but rather us believing lies that has caused us to be far less expectant, believing, and cooperative with the present supernatural activity of heaven. But this is changing for you, even now, as you are trusting the Holy Spirit to break down these strongholds and lead you into the freedom you've been qualified to experience since the victory of the cross. It is amazing that truth really does set us free.

I want to transition into some personal experiences I've had, in order to provoke you to hunger. May I remind you these experiences are nothing I earned by any superior spiritual disciplines. This entire spiritual realm of God has been opened to us in a way unlike ever before, solely through the paid price of Jesus blood. However, dispelling the lies that have obstructed our personal experiencing of that reality, allows us to practically begin experiencing these birthrights of ours. That truly has been the only difference for me when comparing most of my life where I didn't have interaction or supernatural encounters, versus the present, where it has become more and more common. In light of that, the Holy Spirit just impressed me to lead you into praying this prayer out loud as we transition to some of these experiences:

Father, I want to experience all that You have given us through the blood of Jesus. I don't want to settle for a powerless Gospel. I don't want to cling to any lies or deceptions I may have unknowingly or knowingly clung to in my religious life. I want to experience You as I've read and heard my whole life from other people's experience in the Scriptures. I want to renounce the lie that your present, supernatural activity is not for me. I want to trust Holy Spirit to be my helper, guide, and comforter as I allow Him to lead me into the territories I have been afraid to believe in or even explore up to now, in fear of being deceived. I want to acknowledge He is more than capable of helping me discern Your ways and voice, and to tear down any low ceilings and walls I've contained you in, so that I may freely begin to operate as a son/daughter of the all-powerful living God that you are. In Jesus' name, Amen.

One of my first encounters with Angelic activity, was when I was approaching the last week of a thirty-day fast. This fast was one in which God had led me to in relation to wanting to be more aligned with Him for the experiencing of greater intimacy with Him. He brought that conviction during the month of Thanksgiving, my favorite meal of the entire year. And anyone that knows me knows I love to eat and I eat well. Only the authentic experiencing of God could have put in me the desire strong enough to follow that conviction even through this annual meal my mother, from out of state, would be cooking. We were driving back from Tennessee at night, and both my wife and son were asleep. All of a sudden, in the upper left corner of my windshield, up in the sky I saw a very bright light, similar to lightning, but in the form of a large ball illuminated very brightly (to where the headlights from the oncoming traffic literally dimmed in comparison), and then shrank down to a smaller ball, and fell down to the earth.

I thought that was crazy enough and wondered, "Wow, what in the world was that all about?" Shortly after seeing this, I glanced up at my rear view mirror, and saw, directly in the middle of the back seat and staring back at me, a male being. He had a slightly darker complexion than I do, he wore glasses as well as a grin, as if knowing I'd be shocked to see him there.

After glancing back to the road and then back in the mirror, he was gone. I remember being so thrown off and wondering, "If that was an angel, why did he have glasses? Don't they have perfect vision?" Well, after further prayer, the Lord showed me this visitation was to show me God was now taking me into greater visions/visuals related to the kingdom, hence the glasses. Glasses help enhance one's vision in the areas they lack.

Sure enough, shortly after this encounter, I began to "see" more things as spiritual dreams, visions, and other physical evidences of angelic activity. These evidences became more and more noticeable and tangible in my practical life. I pray for more and more to increase; it is extremely exciting to explore the many ways our heavenly Father loves to communicate with us.

I pray even now for you to take a moment to gaze into heaven, and also ask for an increase and greater awareness of what your heavenly Father is doing all around you, as it's His intention to reveal them to you more and more every day. Pray that unbelief, skepticism, and faulty thought patterns may be shaken off you and your capacity to receive more of His present activity in your life, in Jesus' name.

A couple of weeks ago, I was talking to my good friend, Kevin Becker, on the phone, and as usual, we were sharing testimonies we've seen or heard of, new revelations or encounters, that stirred each other up for experiencing *more* of God.

This time he said, "Hey, when we connect again we should do some praying."

I remember thinking, "Huh, I wonder what God is up to for him to say that." Well in a couple of hours, we reconnected and he asked me what I wanted prayer for. I said, "I feel that when it comes to God's voice, whether it be through signs and wonders or other ways He speaks, that I've been so fear-stricken of the devil's counterfeits my whole life, that I automatically default to giving him credit rather than defaulting to giving God credit. I feel like, at the root of that, I just don't believe my heavenly Father can be that good to give me such communication regularly, and I'm tired of that obstructing me from hearing what He's saying to me. I feel like it keeps interfering from me hearing His voice."

So, he prayed for me and after praying, he said, "I declare those obstructions are now a thing of the past, in Jesus' name. I declare they are behind you. You are not that person anymore, so don't even acknowledge it as a part of who you are, because it's not you now. You are made new, and ever ready to hear from your Father, expectant and believing in His goodness and ability to do so."

I declared in agreement, "I receive it in Jesus' name." Well, later that night, I found this short clip on YouTube (*God's Spokesman*, by Art Katz), talking about how imperative it is for us to hear from God before trying to declare His Word, and I thought, "Man, this is so profound and aligned with what we were discussing today." So, I sent it to Kevin saying, "It is so imperative we are hearing God's voice."

As I got ready to fall asleep, I prayed, "Lord, I thank you for what you're doing. I thank you for clearer hearing, and more attentive ears, in Jesus' name. I pray for your angels to just mess with me tonight." Then I put in my earplugs (which, at the time, I used overnight) and fell asleep. Around the time I usually get up, I notice I was hearing noises in the room and in the house that I normally wouldn't be able to hear with my earplugs in. I realized they weren't in my ears anymore. I thought it was a bit strange and then thought, "Ah, man, wouldn't it be cool if my angel put them neatly on my nightstand or something." I looked around for them in my bed, then glanced down at the floor, expecting to see one somewhere in the bed sheets and the other some other random place, but instead when I sat up, I noticed they were neatly put together, both facing the same direction, directly on the bed where the center of my back had been resting. They were both still squeezed from me laying on them and had begun to regain their form. From the intentional positioning of them, I was instantly aware there had been some angelic activity to cause this. I've had ear plugs fall out in the past and, when they do, they are never found close to one another, and never once anything even remotely like this.

I laughed and then asked God to bring me understanding of what this meant. I've learned that signs and wonders aren't just random and for no reason. *They always have an intentional purpose and carry the voice of God through them, if we press on to understand beyond the initial awe of the sign/wonder.* Shortly after, the Lord brought my memory back to the previous day, where Kevin had declared that the "Obstructions hindering me from hearing God's voice were now behind me and a thing of the past." Well, what do earplugs do? Obstruct your ears to hear. They were placed behind my back signifying the obstructions were now "behind me and a thing of the past." Then, I also remembered that, just before bed, I had asked for the angels to "just mess with me" and so they did.

God's voice is so diverse in how He communicates with us. If we'd only believe in His ability to speak to us so practically and lovingly, we'd really experience so much more intimacy with Him in such real ways. I'm so humbled more and more in my walk with Him, as I'm discovering He speaks to us far more frequently than we even realize. It's no wonder the enemy doesn't want us to tune in. God's voice becomes the one thing you will desire to hear more; with it, there truly is abundant life imparted. His *daily bread* is truly the depositing of His present presence into our lives, as He is so intricately and intimately involved and interested in everything we do and everything we are.

A great resource that has blessed me is a book called, *God of Wonders* by Brian Guerin, where he touches on the biblical ways God operated in this manner, and personal testimonies of modern-day experiences modeling the same thing. His ministry, "Bridal Glory International" has greatly blessed me and my growing intimacy with Jesus. Like several other resources the Lord has recently brought into my life, he is about one thing: intimacy with Jesus. From there flows everything.

Recently I was heading to a meeting, about an hour away from my house, and had to make a quick stop at my office downtown to print some paperwork from my computer for the meeting. I remember since it was going to be quick, I didn't bring in my laptop bag (I left it in in the back seat) and just brought my keys and the sunglasses I'd been wearing. When I opened the office, I set my keys and sunglasses on the desk as usual, printed off what I needed, and then rushed downstairs and back to my car. After driving for just a few minutes, the glare of the Florida sun hit my eyes, I reached to put on my sunglasses and realized I'd left them on my desk. I thought, "Oh, man. It's so bright, too." I considered going back to get them since I still had another thirty to forty-minute drive ahead but the sun hit me square in the face. Checking the time, I knew I'd be late if I went back.

So, the whole drive, I kept thinking, "Man I can't believe I left them. Wow, it's so bright out." (I know... what a diva *right*?) Well, I got to the meeting and forgot about the sun and the sunglasses. I was using my laptop, so I removed it along with the bulky, box-like plug from the front pocket of the bag. When we finished, about three hours later, I unplugged the laptop and, after wrapping up the cord, unzipped the front pocket to put it back inside. And low and behold, what do I see right there inside of that front pocket of the bag? My sunglasses. I was so thrown off, first of all, because I'm very intentional where I put my glasses, especially since one of the lenses pops out all the time (I've had them for over ten years) and I've never and would never place them in this computer bag, especially under that heavy box plug. I had a human moment and thought, "Did I put them there while rushing out of the office?" But then I remembered, "How could I, when that bag stayed in the car for the ten minutes I had rushed in and out of the office."

So, there would be no way for the sunglasses to have been put there by my hands in the office. It took me a little while to sink it all in after replaying that morning in my head and ruling out any other possibilities, to finally accept the only possibility left – which was angelic assistance sent by my loving, heavenly Father, who'd care about something so little as this. How special this made me feel. He loves to shower us with His loving reminders of just how good, He practically is.

Another time, right before leaving my house for work, I placed my wallet on a shelf near the bathroom sink. I *never* place it there and even said out loud, "Watch you'll forget it, since you never put it there." Sure enough, I left for work and when I was just minutes from my office, I remembered that I didn't grab my wallet. I put my hand into my left pocket where I usually kept it, felt around, and emptied it only to find my cell phone and business card holder. *No wallet.*

I remember saying, "Man. I knew I'd forget it because I never put it there." I told my boss and fellow director, who were both visiting for the day, that I had left my wallet at home. When I got to work, right before exiting my car, I took out my business card holder and left it in the car for later, so the only thing remaining in that pocket was my cell phone. All morning I reached into my left pocket to use my phone for calls, text messages, and emails. Still no wallet. I got into my friend's car to go on a visit to a referral source, but after feeling around in my pocket again, I realized I needed to get my business card holder from my car.

"Hey, let me get my business card holder from my car really quick." So, I got to my car, put it into my left pocket and we went on our way. After our meeting, we walked out from the building, talking. When I reached into my left pocket, low and behold my wallet was suddenly there. In disbelief, I pulled it out. Astonished, I said out loud, "What the heck?"

My friend said, "Cool man, there it is."

I was still amazed. "But, it wasn't there all morning." As I recounted the numerous steps of the morning, the small size of the pocket, how many times I'd emptied it, checked it, and used it all morning with no wallet present, I knew this was another instance of angelic assistance. This has continued to happen with other things and, each time, I just laugh to myself because I still find myself trying to find some *normal* explanation for the occurrence. Every time, after ruling out the natural possibilities, I've been left to just believe and receive the divine assistance. Anyone who knows me, knows I'm not the type to forget things, like where I placed my keys. In fact, I'm very intentional with personal belongings, which is why, even in these instances, it wasn't that I didn't know where I'd placed the sunglasses or wallet. I knew exactly where I had left them – the sunglasses were on my office desk and the wallet was left on a bathroom shelf near the sink.

But I guess I never thought God would orchestrate angels to assist with such little things. From my previous religious perspective, those type of things wouldn't be important enough or spiritual enough of a reason for God to send angels to assist. But I've realized over time that thought processes like trying to rationalize God's help is nothing more than the religious reasoning's of man. I've found that God cares for us, even in the smallest things. If you're a parent, you wouldn't hesitate to help your little one in any and every way possible. Wouldn't a God of love do exceedingly more?

I hope you're starting to see why I'm so crazily passionate for us to believe in the present presence and voice of our LIVING GOD. It so imperative we are growing with, walking with, and experiencing

Him the way He has always intended – and stop believing the lies for anything less practical and real. Lord, quicken our senses and hearts.

> "But who [among them] has stood in the council *(intimate place)* of the LORD,
> That he would *perceive (see)* and *hear* His word?
> Who has marked His word [noticing and observing and paying attention to it] and has [actually] heard it?" Jeremiah 23:18 AMP (Italicized emphasis mine=Greek)

CHAPTER 7

MAN'S SPIRIT UNITED WITH GOD'S

Whenever I was left unsure of a supernatural testimony I'd heard, God would tell me, "If it's from Me, you will surely experience the same and more if you prioritize your time and life with Me as they have." And I have found this to be very true. If you prioritize the secret place of intimacy with Jesus, (not just a devotion time you check off) you will find your life and your house one that heaven loves to "break into" with supernatural encounters and revelations. It's inevitable. The majority of the supernatural activity from God, is the byproduct of intimacy with Jesus. Anything less, no matter how impressive to mankind, is void of heaven's recognition in the final judgment according (see Matthew 7:21-23).

Something I began to learn was that I had believed, and even made up, various faulty conclusions to explain or reason away why I wasn't walking out the supernatural yet (along with many other fellow believers). These lies were my way of coping with the Scriptures that clearly spoke on the practical supernatural lifestyle of the believer. "When the Lord is ready, He'll send the Latter Rain, but until then we'll just keep waiting for it," was what I believed. It's much easier for us to believe that, because it makes us feel better than realizing something on our end is the problem. The more I heard of the miracles and breakthroughs happening in various places and ministries, the more challenged I felt to explain them away. That's why it's easier for the "flesh" to avoid such ministries and places. Upon some serious introspection, I had to come to the sobering reality that the problem wasn't on God's end. He wasn't and isn't being stingy with the Holy Spirit. In fact, "If you then, who are evil, know how to give good gifts to your children, *how much more will* the heavenly Father *give the Holy Spirit to those who ask Him.*" Lk.11:13.

I soon began to learn that asking Him meant more than saying the words, "Lord, we want the Holy Spirit." Many people and churches have asked, saying those words while still remaining unchanged, powerless, and absent of the supernatural presence and power of the Holy Spirit. The Greek word here actually means to "crave, desire." When a man craves or desires a particular woman to be his spouse, it's a burning desire to pursue her, despite whatever challenges, and not settle for anything or anyone else. Many people today ask for the Holy Spirit verbally but have no craving for His presence. They more often crave the honor of men, their pastor, church officials, a pulpit, recognition, ministry endorsements, validation of others, the praise of others, or clothing themselves in a form of godliness, while clearly void of heaven's endorsing presence/power. But when studying any modern-day revival – Asuza Street revival (1906), Brownsville revival (mid 90s) and many others, you'll find, prior to the outpouring of the Holy Spirit, was a man, woman, or small group of men and women who were tired of the earthly validations and sought more than anything else with a growing craving – heaven's validation and endorsement, regardless of the cost. It wasn't just a weekly attendance to a building. It was often seven days a week, many hours per day individually and collectively, perusing their craving, the presence of the living God. "For He that comes to God must believe that He is, and that He is a rewarder to those who diligently seek Him." Hebrews 11:6. Notice, when we "come to God," we must believe that HE IS. Not just believing He WAS (past tense) or believing He will be (future), but believing HE IS (present tense). His presence is of highest importance to everything we believe and do, as Christian believers.

If you came from a religious background like I did, you've learned very well how to approach the written Word of God for devotion time, to study who He was throughout Scripture. You've learned who He will be in the future when He comes back to take us home with Him. But have you encountered the tangible presence of the present living Christ lately? Or was your last transforming encounter with Him the very first time you met Him – at your conversion?

I never realized how much Jesus longs for us to encounter His presence daily. In any close human relationship, it is considered healthy to express love through a physical hug, even several times a day. Yet, when it comes to Jesus and the Holy Spirit, we often shun the invitation of any sort of physical manifestation from God, because we simply don't believe Him to be that real or interested in relating to us in a physical way. Instead, have you thought or heard anyone comment something to this effect: "I'm mature in my study of the Scriptures, and therefore don't need any type of goosebumps, tingling, or whatever physical reassurance from God, because I have His written Word." Such statements are typically made from a false humility and, if you dig deeper, what they are truly saying is, "I've never personally experienced God's tangible presence, and in fact, I'm scared to because I don't want to be deceived by any demonic new age stuff, so this is how I play it safe," The person is, therefore, comfortably insulated by unbelief.

I totally understand the fear. This was my theological position my entire life until I just couldn't ignore all of the supernatural experiences which are recorded throughout both the Old and New Testaments any longer. Seriously, have you read them lately? The numerous encounters of angels appearing with messages, Jesus and His disciples and, later on, Philip teleporting from one location to another from over thirty miles away – in an instant. There are records of spiritual dreams and encounters with the supernatural, people falling over – appearing drunk – because their physical bodies couldn't with stand the degree of power felt by Holy Spirit's presence (Acts 2), and so many others. There are so many wild and humanly irrational experiences and encounters in the Bible that remain represented as mere fairy tales to us, until we awaken to the reality that He hasn't changed. And, in fact, the cross of Christ has opened that realm to us in ways unavailable to previous generations. So, why would we remain ignorant and reject the incredible, experiential, real, and adventurous divine birthright He died to give us? We have exchanged God's truth and reality for Satan's lies of powerless religious garb, crippling God's children from the truth as it is in Jesus.

I remember one morning, while in my secret place, I had just finished telling Jesus how I felt so discouraged and disheartened. Then immediately after, I saw an image of Jesus standing on an ocean in front of me, smiling a big smile. He laughed with joy as He caused the waves to crash over me. As they stuck me, I could feel the tangible warmth of His love saturate me. Such an experience caused me to physically bow down before Him in a way I'd yet to experience. I felt as if I had to bow due to His overwhelming presence, and yet felt like my bowing on the floor still wasn't low enough to express how I felt at that moment.

His presence came into the room so tangibly that it literally shifted the atmosphere while causing an overwhelming presence to come over me beyond the point of tears. I was a mess, with snot and endless tears pouring down from my face as all I could do was just sob and sob. Can you imagine how the rest of my day went after this encounter? Do you think I had trouble staying focused on the things of God, resisting temptation for secular things? No way. How could I?

There is nothing this world can offer that is even close to the present presence and voice of the living God. Nothing. I'm fully convinced that at the root of every distracted soul, both inside and outside of the church, is a lack of experiencing the living Christ. The God who IS.

All throughout scripture, you see the immediate and long-term effects on the lives of men and women, despite years of affliction, torment, disease, hurt, and pain, who were forever changed by just one touch from Jesus. Who else is like Him? "Come to Him believing HE IS; diligently seek Him" and watch how quickly His life will consume yours.

Have you settled for a much more stoic, intangible God, who finds such practical encounters as spiritually immature or unnecessary as many religious people teach? We often reject what we don't understand or what we haven't personally experienced, instead of pressing into Him for understanding and revelation on such things. We all quickly acknowledge the numerous tangible ways the demonic realm operates, yet we allow the absence of our own tangible encounters with God to shape a theology that can explain our lack of such experiences. But what if we aligned our thinking with what God's Word shows us about His tangibility throughout the ages, despite what we've personally experienced?

As I spent more time in the secret place, He began to activate something deep within me that I didn't know needed activation. You see, I had spent my entire church and ministry life viewing God as one I could engage with theologically with my mind and mind alone. I loved the written Word of God but was clueless of His spoken word and present voice. In fact, we celebrated how theologically sound we were compared to other churches and other Christians. Yet what I had developed was religious pride, arrogance, and a false sense of security that quenched the active Spirit of God from having more possession of me.

God wanted to break me away from everything and anything that was in His position, the places He belonged. Things I'd subconsciously put my security in, He wanted to exchange those things for Himself. My spiritual assessment of myself for His. His way of engaging with His presence instead of what I believed to be the way. In essence, a fuller yes and a fuller surrender to Him than ever before.

In John, chapter 4, Jesus was speaking with the woman at the well. The subject of worship to God comes up as the woman makes the following statement in verse 20:

> ²⁰Our fathers worshiped in this mountain, and you *people* (Jews) say that in Jerusalem is the place where men ought to worship." ²¹Jesus said to her, "Woman, believe Me, an hour is coming when neither in this mountain nor in Jerusalem will you worship the Father. ²²You worship what you do not know; we worship what we know, for salvation is from the Jews. ²³ But an hour is coming, and now is, when the <u>true worshipers</u> will worship the Father in <u>spirit and truth</u>; for such people the Father seeks to be His worshipers. ²⁴*God is spirit*, and those who worship Him *must worship in spirit and truth*."
>
> Hebrews 9:1 NASB says, "Now even the first *covenant* had regulations of divine <u>worship</u> and the earthly sanctuary...."

The word *worship* is one I thought meant what we do during music service, but it goes much deeper than this and actually means a "reverence, adoring, and surrendering to/rendering one as superior to yourself." Oftentimes in Scripture, it is contextually implying a communing/engaging with God. There is a huge difference on how humans could commune and engage with God *before* Jesus died on the cross and *after*. Hence, why I quoted Hebrews 9:1 after this verse. Without understanding exactly what has changed and how it's changed, we could be believing that we have to connect/engage with God in the same limited manner and ways the people of the

Old Testament did, rather than the supernatural ways Jesus died to give us. I've found the more understanding and belief I have of the Gospel, the more intimacy with God I experience in true worship.

Before sin, man was used to a very tangible, practical, real, walking with God experience. (Genesis 3:8). The presence of God was the very life-giving source in which we were in perfect alignment with and could have chosen to never depart from Him. However, we all know the story from Genesis, chapter 3, and how we chose to depart from the tangible presence of God, and, in fact, sin caused us to even fear it (See Gen. 3:10). It's no coincidence that, at the root of every religious skepticism of the supernatural operating today, is the fear of being deceived. Remember this: the devil's primary objective is to keep us from a present tense, practical, real, walking/communing with the living God.

Those who merely talk about God who "once walked with man" or who "will one day walk with man" aren't much of a threat to the enemy as they aren't utilizing any of the available divine power and authority. But those who *are walking* with the empowering presence and voice of God and releasing that same power and presence into the lives of the people in their path, (causing true supernatural deliverance, freedom, and breakthroughs to take place), are those the devil fears. He fears them because they know their redeemed identity and have embraced the reality of the Son of God being alive inside of them to do His *supernatural* works through them.

Since the fall of man, we've tried to fill our void with any and everything else and have failed. Outside of God's presence, we have no peace, life, love, joy, or eternal substance. At the center of our very DNA is the place for which only God's presence fits, and no other counterfeit can impart the quality of abundant life like He does. The Old Testament shows us the "closest" man could get to a Holy God after sin and prior to the cross of Christ, and it wasn't very close.

God gave them various methods, sacrifices, laws and rituals, as *symbols* to put their trust and faith in the coming Savior Jesus, who would *one day* bring humanity back into a *living experiencing* of God's presence. But these practices and traditions became a stumbling block, and God's people put their reliance on these works rather than in Him.

If you read Exodus, Deuteronomy, and Leviticus, you'll find many laws, rules, requirements that are focused on the physical body and physical realm, as they were designed to meet the condition of unredeemed man at the time. They emphasize on what you need to abstain and refrain from in order to remain *clean*. But unfortunately, they were just symbolic practices of the actual practical cleansing of sin Jesus's sacrifice of Himself would give us (we briefly touched on that in an earlier chapter). In reference to this old order, the scripture says,

> "Accordingly both gifts and sacrifices are offered which *cannot* make the *worshiper* perfect in conscience, ¹⁰ since they *relate* only to food and drink and various washings, *regulations for the body* imposed *until a time of reformation*."–Hebrews 9:9-10 NASB

The Amplified version, (which supplies further elaboration in brackets from the Greek translation and context) says:

> ⁹"for this [first or outer tabernacle] is a symbol [that is, an archetype or paradigm] for the present time. Accordingly, both gifts and sacrifices are offered which are incapable of perfecting the conscience *and* renewing the [inner self of the] worshiper. ¹⁰For they [the gifts, sacrifices, and ceremonies] deal only with [clean and unclean] food and drink and various ritual washings, *[mere]* external regulations for the body *imposed [to help the worshipers] until the time of reformation [that is, the time of the new order when Christ will establish the reality of what these things foreshadow—a better covenant]."

The cross of Christ, His blood and His blood alone, was an absolute must, in order to reconcile or bring back into divine union, man, and God. "⁴For it is impossible for the blood of bulls and goats to take away sins." Hebrews 10:4 NASB. This is why a true indwelling connection with the presence of God couldn't take place *until* His blood was shed.

So back to John 4 (the woman at the well), Jesus was explaining to this woman that, despite the Jews "knowing what they worship" (Jews were considered most knowledgeable of the things of God, since God had given them sanctuary practices, regulations etc.), even their worship would be *superseded* by what He, Himself was introducing in "this very hour." What was Jesus introducing? T*rue worship* not only of truth but of *spirit and truth*. Well, why would that be important? Because "God is spirit and those who worship Him <u>must</u> worship in spirit and in truth." (Jn 4:24) Let's unpack this:

In all of the Old Testament stories, up to the cross of Christ, mankind was spiritually dead, trying to worship and commune with a God who is spirit. This disconnect between God and man is better understood when we understand how God originally made us to connect with Him, Spirit to spirit.

²³"Now may the God of peace Himself sanctify you *entirely*; and may *your spirit* and *soul* and *body* be preserved complete, without blame at the coming of our Lord Jesus Christ. 1Thessolonians 5:23 NASB

> Notice the writer is referring to our *entirety* as three parts: body, soul, and spirit. The word *soul* in the original language refers to our mind/our will, where we make decisions and choices. The *body* is the physical part of us that carries out what the *soul* or mind tells it to do. But what function or role does our *spirit* have? And what does the Bible say about it?

When God told Adam in Gen. 2:17, "The day you eat of the tree you will surely die," He wasn't joking. But yet, we see Adam still *physically* living after he ate of the tree and sinned, but we don't see His spirit capable of engaging with the "God who is spirit" after that point. This is evidenced by the immediate disconnect with the presence of God, and the obvious absence of it in the following chapters.

Man's spirit, which was designed to be engaged with and united together with God's Spirit, was now void of life as it was severed from God's Holy Spirit. So, man could only relate to a God of spirit, with just his body and soul (mind/will) from that point on. This is why everything given to man from God after this point in scripture, was always focused on *physical* things that man could relate to such as sacrificing an animal, sprinkling the blood here, putting this over there, not touching this, but touching that instead. These were physical rituals to help man relate to the spiritual connection/worship Jesus would one day restore through His blood sacrifice on the cross.

They were "regulations *of the body* imposed <u>until</u> a time of reformation," as Hebrews 9:9-10 said.

I never understood what is the "spirit of man" mentioned throughout Scripture. I would read that verse in 1 Thess. 5:23; we read earlier and interpreted the word "spirit" to mean "Holy Spirit." However, why would the Holy Spirit need to be "preserved complete and without blame" upon Jesus return when He is already and always has been? I had also believed when the "spirit of man" was mentioned, it was just referring to the "breath of man." But once again, this Scripture, along with many others (look it up for yourself), doesn't warrant that interpretation in the context it is written. Contextually, we are left to accept that the "entirety" or "complete" man is three-fold – *spirit*, *soul* and *body* – and the good news is that God has restored perfect redemption to all three areas. We were created in the image and likeness of the Godhead, according to Genesis 1:26. When we look at the roles of the Father, Son, and Holy Spirit, we see how our soul, body, and spirit reflect the way the three of them are.

For example: Look at our *soul*, where our mind/will/decision making is. Just as God the Father is mentioned as the one who sent His Son to the world; it was the *Father's will* Jesus said He had come to make known and reveal to us. Our *body* is made like God the Son, Jesus, as He was made *flesh/a body* and dwelt among us (Jn 1:14). Our *spirit* is made like the Holy Spirit of God. Holy Spirit doesn't have physical flesh, but He carries the very desires and heart of the Father, and as Holy Spirit possessed Jesus' body here on earth, He fulfilled the Father's will through Jesus body. In the same way scripture says of our spirit,

> [11] For who among men knows the *thoughts* of a man except the *spirit of the man which is in him?* Even so the *thoughts* of God no one knows except the Spirit of God. -1 Corinthians 2:11

> The *spirit of man* is the lamp of the LORD, Searching all the innermost parts of his (man's) being. Proverbs 20:27 (my parenthesis)

> Behold, You desire truth in the *innermost being*, And in the *hidden part* You will make me know wisdom. Psalms 51:6

Restoring our spiritual, Spirit-to-spirit connection with God has been His goal from the moment sin severed it. It has also been the devil's objective to keep us ignorant and void of the full realities of this truth.

Can you imagine if one of the Godhead were absent or out of alignment with the others? Yet as you will see, that is exactly what the devil targeted to do to our spirit/inner most being, which of course then affected our mind and body too. Watch how scripture highlights the role of our spirit in relation to the New Covenant order Jesus has given us for our re-union with "God who is spirit" to be possible:

> "The Spirit Himself testifies with *our spirit* that we are children of God..." Romans 8:16

> Notice *how* the Holy Spirit testifies, and bears witness of our new redeemed identities as Children of the living God-*with our spirit*.

> "...that He would grant you, according to the riches of His glory, to be strengthened with *power* through His Spirit *in* the *inner man*..." Ephesians 3:16 (New Testament has several other verses referring to our spirit as "the new man, inner man, new self)."

> The riches of His glory are revealed through our lives *as* we are empowered by the Holy Spirit in our inner man.

> [16] Or do you not know that the one who joins himself to a prostitute is one body *with her*? For He says, "THE TWO SHALL BECOME ONE FLESH." [17] But the one who joins himself to the Lord is *one spirit with Him*." 1Corithians 6:17 NASB.

Scripture says we (the church) are the bride of Christ. This is because the intimate nearness of a husband and wife, is the closest symbolic relationship to the spiritual union between the spirit of man and the Spirit of God becoming one. This is true worship. Apart from this union, we could never be a suitable bride to Jesus. But because of His blood and the gift of this spiritual union we are a Holy reflection of the God in whose image we were created. This was Jesus very prayer right before He went to the cross:

> [20] "I do not ask on behalf of these alone, but for those also who believe in Me through their word; [21] that they may all be *one*; *even as* You, Father, *are* in Me and I in You, that they also may be in Us, so that the world may believe that You sent Me." John 17:20-21 NASB.

"You IN me and I IN YOU?" How were Jesus and the Father "one" while He was physically down here? They were united in Spirit, therefore, Jesus was possessed by the very Spirit and presence of the living God. How was Jesus able to carry out the will of the Father? The supernatural works of the Father? The supernatural love of the Father? By the very Spirit of the Father that was inside of Him. However, Jesus didn't just model what "*the* Son of God" looks like and lives like, but what "*A* Son of the living God" looks like and lives like. That's why the Bible refers to Him as the "firstborn among many brethren," -Romans 8:29. That word, "firstborn," in the original language, comes from the same word we get "prototype" from. Notice how the verses below refer to us who have now been redeemed or bought back:

[14] For all who are being led by the Spirit of God, these are sons of God. [15] For you have not received a spirit of slavery leading to fear again, but you have received a spirit of adoption as sons by which we cry out, "Abba. Father." [16] The Spirit Himself testifies with our spirit that we are children of God, [17] and if children, heirs also, heirs of God and *fellow heirs* with Christ, if

indeed we suffer with *Him* so that we may also be glorified with *Him*." -Romans 8:14-17 NASB

How are sons of God led? By the Spirit of God. But how does a Spirit truly *lead* someone? In the physical realm, if you were leading a child across a busy road, you would grab their physical hand with yours to do so. Your hand and theirs would be connecting you both. But the physical realm and spiritual are not the same, which is why the Holy Spirit leads a person by their spirit.

You've probably read the conversation between Jesus and a religious leader named Nicodemas written in John chapter 3. But if you're anything like me, you've also probably missed what Jesus was truly explaining to him which is directly about this topic.

Jesus tells Nicodemas in John 3:3 that "Unless one is born again he cannot see the Kingdom of God." Nicodemas is baffled at such a statement because he is viewing it in terms of physical birth from a physical body, hence, why he responds to Jesus in vs. 4 with, "How can a man be born when he is old? He cannot enter a second time into his mother's womb and be born, can he?" Jesus then responds with this in vs. 5-8:

> "Truly, truly, I say to you, unless one is born of water and the Spirit (some versions say, "from above") he cannot enter into the kingdom of God. ⁶That which is born of the flesh is flesh, and *that which is born of the Spirit is spirit.* ⁷Do not be amazed that I said to you, 'You must be born again.'⁸ The wind blows where it wishes and you hear the sound of it, but do not know where it comes from and where it is going; *so is everyone who is born of the Spirit."* (John 3:3-8)

The "New Birth" produced by the Gospel (Good News) of Jesus Christ is not just a moral exchange of your past bad morals and habits for some new ones. It's a surrendering up of the very nature and order we lived under and with our whole lives till this point. The nature that was spiritually dead, and therefore unable to connect or be one with God. It's an exchange, being "born again," not of the flesh like from an earthly Mother, but from the very Spirit of the living God as He births in us a new spirit — a new receiving capacity for Him to fill, dwell, and lead us with. (If you read the scriptures on baptism and the Spirit led life such as Romans 6, 8, and John 3, you'll see just how clearly scripture speaks on this)

> "Therefore if anyone is in Christ, *he is* a new creature; the old things passed away; behold, new things have come." 2 Corinthians 5:17 NASB

One of the biggest deceptions the enemy has thrived on for years, is keeping the people of God entertained with the traditions, theologies, programs, and the busyness of religion, while remaining spiritually restricted. It's no wonder so many of us professed Christians have such a lack of supernatural power and presence of the Holy Spirit. It is form of godliness, only without power. Did the ministry and life of Jesus or the early-church believers ever succumb to such a staleness and lack of God's living proofs for today? No way. But we've ignored the obvious elephant in the room for so much and for so long that enough of us have learned to live with it there and have formulated theologies, explanations, and theories to explain ourselves away from the truth of the Gospel, and into blatant unbelief.

The popular religious lifestyle so often called "Christianity" in our modern world, is a far cry from the *spiritual life* that the Biblical Christian modeled. Jesus' death restored to us access to being one in Spirit with God and to rule and reign co-laboring with Him to destroy the works of the devil on this earth, *just as Jesus and the apostles modeled* (in fact, even more so). The spiritual life modeled in Scripture is exciting, engaging, real, tangible, powerful, thrilling, and unlike anything else in the world. This redeemed spiritual life is not limited to the physical laws and realm like our body is.

Jesus modeled this in the numerous examples such as, walking on water, teleporting himself and a boat of disciples across a lake, and many other examples in scripture. Our citizenship truly is from heaven now. This is the good news. The last thing the devil wants is more and more people realizing the priceless inheritance the Son of God has so graciously given us.

Pray this out loud with me:

Father, I pray you expand my horizon beyond my comfort zone. Please pull me in closer for a deeper connection with You. I pray You give me peace to entrust myself to Your Holy Spirit, whom you've promised would be my guide into ALL truth. Help me to believe more in Your abilit to lead me than the devil's ability to deceive me, in Jesus' name, Amen.

CHAPTER 8

FUEL THE INNER SPIRIT MAN

When you were younger, do you remember those T.V.s that had just two knobs? They each had a set number of channels printed on the knobs and you would change the channel by turning the knob. (I'm not that old, but my grandmother had one of these.) Before we are spiritually born again, we are like this T.V. We have a body just like the T.V. has a physical encasing. We have a soul/mind where decisions are made, just like the knobs of the T.V. are turned to choose what channel to turn to. But our spirit was lifeless just like a T.V. without an antenna. Without an antenna on the T.V., you would find yourself turning and turning the knobs, with little to no reception or connection to any channel being broadcast into the air-waves. And so it is, when our spirit man is dead or not positioned to receive the leading of the tangible Holy Spirit, we are simply turning our "knobs," striving with our own efforts, trying to connect with a God who is spirit. Our *screen,* or life, displays what we are receiving, and if what we are receiving isn't coming in clear, the picture is fuzzy and the sound distorted or even absent altogether.

Although there are many air waves of broadcasting being put out into the atmosphere, (just as God is always speaking to us) the connection with those air waves depends on how well the T.V. can receive them. Like the knobs and the physical components of the T.V. housing the screen, this is how we are before we receive the resto-ration of our spirit via union of His Spirit with ours. We are a body (physical components of the T.V.) and mind (knobs), displaying on the screen (our life) a fuzzy picture of the supernatural nature, pres-ence, and power of almighty God. We can preach to people all day long about what our "user manual," or Bible, says about Him, but they are looking for the tangible evidence of Him – His supernatural presence to display on our screen.

After all, don't we say the Holy Spirit lives inside of us? When the Holy Spirit births a new spirit in us, and we get baptized and fully submerged with His Spirit in ours, it's as if Holy Spirit gives us an antenna that can catch the signal that heaven has been putting out the whole time. This antenna, our spirit, is specifically designed to receive the *airwaves* or presence and voice of God. It is then and only then that a clear picture of the present presence and voice of God is displayed on the screens of our lives. It is then and only then that what we read in the manual (Bible) comes into living, practical, reality. But what would happen if once you got that antenna someone took it from off of the top of the T.V (where it belongs) and put it under the T.V? The reception would get fuzzy once again. Even after you have an antenna, you still have to learn how to position it to catch certain channels. You probably remember going to someone's house and saying, "Hey, you don't get channel 5 here?" and they'd respond with, "Yeah, hold on, you have to move this right antenna rod all the way down here and this one over here." And sure enough, channel 5 would then come in clearly because *they knew how to receive it.*

So much of the Gospel from the beginning and into eternity, is *experienced* by receiving all that our heavenly Father has done, is doing, and will be doing. *"All spiritual blessings have already been given to us in Christ Jesus"* (Eph.1:3) but we only experience and demonstrate them to the degree we have learned *how* to receive them.

Our entire lives before becoming a Christian we were operating much like orphans – lost, confused, and unable to hear the voice of God. We were operating with our soul/mind leading in front, and our body following. Everything was only received by our mind and human reasoning, then relayed to our body. The problem with this "order" (besides the obvious absence of a new spirit) is that God's nature, His ways, His order, is completely contrary to the physical order and mindsets we are born with:

> "For My thoughts are not your thoughts, Nor are your ways My ways," declares the LORD. "For *as* the heavens are higher than the earth, So are My ways higher than your ways, And My thoughts than your thoughts." Isa 55:8-9 NASB.

> [5] For those who are according to the flesh set their minds on the things of the flesh, but those who are according to the Spirit, the things of the Spirit.[6] For the mind set on the flesh is death, but the mind set on the Spirit is life and peace, [7] because the mind set on the flesh is hostile toward God; for it does not subject itself to the law of God, for it is not even able *to do so*, [8] and those who are in the flesh cannot please God." Ro. 8:5-8.

You may be thinking, "Yeah, but that last verse is only talking about the flesh regarding evil works, like murder, etc." But consider this next passage along with this last one and you'll see just how often the writers are contrasting the "old order" (Old Covenant/physical order) vs. the new order (New Covenant/spiritual/kingdom order)

> [16] Therefore from now on we recognize no one according to the *flesh*; even though we have known Christ according to the flesh, yet now we know *Him in this way* no longer. [17] Therefore if anyone is in Christ, *he is* a new creature (or creation); the old things passed away; behold, new things have come. 2Corinthians 5:16,17 NASB Parenthesis mine.

In other words, just as Jesus came in the flesh/body of man and yet is now absent physically but present by the Spirit, so we no longer recognize each other (believers) as in the order of the fleshly body/realm but instead as the new creatures born from above, as spiritual men/women, since "old things have passed away and behold new things have come."

Religious ways are such a counterfeit to the true spiritual life, because it presents a "form of Godliness" that *continues to function and operate under the old physical order*. Religion is extremely intellectually based and, since our old order was the leading of our mind first, body second (and no spirit), we say, "Oh okay, I can do this. Just teach me whatever I need to know (with our mind first and our mind leading) and that is all I need to do." The result? What most of us have lived out for a long time – a polished theology, with all kinds of explanations, yet very little transformational supernatural empowering from heaven. The Israelites in Exodus failed to fulfil God's purpose and promise for their lives because of their captivity under this old order. Under the "old order," one who's spirit is dead like theirs or neglected like many today (religious unbelief places our new antennae under the T.V instead of on top) God is extremely predictable and presented as fully explainable, because in that old order He's no bigger to us than the size of *our* brain, *our* thinking, and *our* reasoning. But in the new order, the mysteries of God that "No eye had seen or ear heard" is NOW available for us through the *new order of the Spirit*, since "the Spirit searches all the thoughts and depths of God." (1Cor.2:9-14). We must allow Holy Spirit to fill our spirit and let Him (Holy Spirit) lead from our spirit being in front, then the mind after, then the body. We have been called by Jesus Himself in Luke 9:23 to "die daily" to self/old order to "follow Jesus" or we can continue doing the religious thing of church programs and rituals while alive in the flesh, but our spirit, deathly ill.

Our God is much bigger than our brains and reasoning which is why only His Spirit can bring us into the greater, inexhaustible depths of His ways. If our mind was how a God who is spirit could be truly received by, there would have been no need for this new order of spiritual life to be given to us.

> "...a natural man does not accept the things of the Spirit of God, for they are foolishness to him; and he cannot understand them, because they are *spiritually* appraised." 1Cor.2:14 NASB.

> [25] "Because the *foolishness of God is wiser than men*, and the weakness of God is stronger than men. [26] For consider your calling, brethren, that there were not many wise according to the flesh, not many mighty, not many noble; [27] but God has chosen the foolish things of the world to shame the wise, and God has chosen the weak things of the world to shame the things which are strong, [28] and the base things of the world and the despised God has chosen, the things that are not, so that He may nullify the things that are, [29] so that no man may boast before God." -1Cor. 1:25-29 NASB.

This is why Jesus says to these pompous, intellectual leaders, "Truly I say to you, unless you are *converted and become like children*, you will not enter the kingdom of heaven. ⁴Whoever then *humbles himself as this child*, he is the greatest in the kingdom of heaven." -Matthew 18:2-4 NASB.

The God of heaven, which men have experienced, testified of in scripture and outside of it, is not one confined by our human intellect. In fact, you'll find as I have, that much of the supernatural kingdom realm is quite offensive to adult-like reasoning and thinking, and often undignified in the eyes of religious people. The things of God's supernatural realm and order are ONLY received, understood, and experienced by the New Covenant order, *the way* Jesus shows us, of a new birth from above, and receiving His new order in place of ours. This is why as our spirit is now leading us, our mind (which is learning to follow after the spirit rather than trying to lead it) needs to be renewed and aligned with the kingdom's order, since it was previously trained by the physical earthly order our whole lives. You'll find, unlike the old order, which was pure intellectual knowledge with minimal practical spirituality and experience, this new order-with our spirit first, mind second, body third, gets developed and nourished in the secret place.

Quality time with Him in intimacy is how our spirit man is led, nourished, fueled and matured. I know, despite how many years I was in the church, preaching, ministering, and giving Bible studies, my spirit man was very diminished and shunned by my religious *mind*set. My preconceptions, rationalizations, and theology, kept everything in order (but the wrong order) for so long, and therefore my "screen," or life, displayed the immaturity of my spirit man, despite how eloquent and biblically educated I believed myself to be along with the applause of my fellow peers.

But as the Holy Spirit continues to fuel your spirit while in His presence, you'll also be led to believers, ministries and resources who are experiencing Him just like you do. You'll find the incredible difference of spirit-filled, presence-centered believers, true spirit-filled worship, and powerful sermons that actually impart His living voice. Your sensitivity will be heightened to anything and anyone filled with His presence as it will nourish your inner man rather than tickle your intellect.

We tend to want some formula or short cut to spiritual growth, hence, why just mentally acknowledging a set of doctrine is so appealing to us, because it's easier to hide our spiritual immaturity behind it. But that's just it. *Heaven has designed things in such a way, that the only way to revive your spirit, to grow and develop him, make him more sensitive to the leading of Holy Spirit, is the practical time we spend in God's presence, namely the secret place.* No formulas or shortcuts.

Those who are quick to oppose this topic of our new spirit inside of us, are typically those who truly haven't surrendered to a presence-centered lifestyle. When we grade our level of spirituality based on what we intellectually know (doctrinally) instead of how we spend our time practically in the secret place and daily life, such teachings like this feel threatening, as it exposes the false security of religion/religious activity we have. If you're anything like me or have experienced something like my religious background, that may resonate with you to some degree or another. But perhaps, even as you've been reading this chapter, you feel His presence tugging at your spirit, provoking you to greater surrender, greater revelation, and greater adventure by surrendering up the controls of your spirituality to Him.

Do you truly believe His Spirit is capable of being your personal guide, teacher, and companion into all the depths of God? Do you believe He is capable of developing, reviving, healing your spirit to being filled with the very Spirit, presence, and power of a supernatural God? To be a man or woman whose life is a walking tabernacle the Spirit of God has been given the right to reign as Lord? There's no formula. No head acknowledgement of a doctrine that you can just theologically accept, while practically remaining outside of tangible experience. He's inviting you to explore the very essence of who He is – the most fascinating person and kingdom in the universe and He's given you the most equipped tour guide possible – the Holy Spirit. But will you surrender the old, fallen physical order in exchange for His?

I challenge you to turn your heart and affections to Him even right now... Just get still and quiet before your heavenly Father, before Jesus, and before Holy Spirit who has been present with you even now... and praying out loud say, *"Holy Spirit, I invite You to submerge my spirit and fill me to overflow; give me Your guidance, comfort, wisdom, discernment, and a childlike faith to receive the supernatural adventures of your Kingdom that Jesus died for me to experience in this abundant life He has given me. Tear down any human, man-made walls in my heart that may be keeping my spirit numb to Yours. Awaken my spirit to become sensitive and receptive to Your tangible presence even right now, in Jesus' name, Amen.*

CHAPTER 9

GOD'S VOICE IN SPIRITUAL DREAMS AND VISIONS

What I began to experience as my time in the secret place continued, and my spirit man continued to grow, was a greater sensitivity to the presence and voice of God in private and public. Being that He died to redeem and restore this divine order back into us, it is His way or *channel* of imparting heavenly realities to us. In other words, as our spirit man is growing and tuning into God's presence in the secret place, we become more aware of God's activity in us and around us because, "God is spirit," and therefore received as such, as we discussed in Chapters 7 and 8.

I began to have spiritual dreams, visions, and supernatural encounters with Him. All throughout Scripture, we read countless accounts of how God communicated His present voice through angels, dreams, visions, miracles, signs, and wonders. Nowhere in the Scripture does it say that the written Word of God (Bible) has taken the place of these means of God's communication. Instead, I've found that the Scriptures *enhance* a clearer framework for His present supernatural communication and, in fact, help lead us into our own experiences with Him.

But the reason it's so popular to believe God doesn't communicate with dreams and visions anymore is because people have twisted the Scriptures to reason out why they aren't having such communication from God. I know this because this is exactly what I did most of my life, along with many leaders of my church. It's much easier for our flesh to say, "I guess He doesn't need to speak to me that way because I have the Bible," than it is to say, "Perhaps I need to grow more spiritually."

We've talked a little on how God uses the angels (Chapter 6) to communicate His present voice and how He still does, but He also uses dreams and visions. In just a few of many examples in scripture below you'll see how often God would use dreams and visions to speak on present matters at hand:

> *Joseph (Genesis 37:1-11):* Joseph's numerous dreams showed him the future when his brothers would one day bow down to him in honor. He also interpreted several unbelievers' dreams including Pharaohs.

> *Solomon (1 Kings 3:5):* God spoke to Solomon in a dream asking him "what would you like for me to give you?" (He asked for supreme wisdom).

> *Daniel (Daniel 2; 4):* Daniel helped the unbelieving King interpret numerous key visions/dreams regarding his kingdom and future prophecies/kingdoms.

> *Joseph (of the New Testament) (Matthew 1:20; 2:13):* Joseph had a dream which helped bring clarity of why his soon to be wife was already pregnant (with Jesus)

> *Cornelius (Acts 10:1-6):* God spoke through a vision to an Italian centurion named Cornelius who desired to know Him. In the vision he was shown where to find the disciple Peter in order for him to come minister to his whole household.

> Notice how even unbelievers had dreams from God. God is communicating so much more to us all than we truly realize and the more we tune into *the ways* He is speaking, the more we will *personally* experience the joy of hearing His voice. Notice how the unbelievers turned to believers to get the interpretation for their dream. What I have found, is the more my spirit man grows in God's presence in the secret place, the more discernment I began to have in understanding my dreams.

If we approach our dreams from our intellect, often they won't make sense to us and we will continue to write them off as random and lack understanding just as an unbeliever would. For me, I never could remember any dreams until my spirit man began to grow. God is spirit, and just like everything else we've been talking about in relation to His present voice, His ways are spiritual. God's will for us as His redeemed sons and daughters, is to *learn from His Spirit how to receive the practical realities of the gospel*. He wants to teach and train us how to hear His present voice so that our lives are in a greater and greater alignment with His *present will* for us.

The enemy, on the other hand, wants to keep us in the mere religious remembering of the "greatest hits" of a God that *once* operated in present supernatural communication with His children, but no longer does. The enemy wants us to believe the lie that God's diverse ways of communicating has lessened rather than increased, in order to drown out His present speaking to us. Despite how popular that lie is in religious circles, the Bible says the complete opposite regarding these *last days* we live in:

> "And it shall come to pass in the last days, says God,
> That I will pour out of My Spirit on all flesh;
>
> Your sons and your daughters shall prophesy, Your young men shall see visions, Your old men shall dream dreams. – Acts 2:17.

My wife actually began to receive spiritual dreams several months before I did. I remember being frustrated because I would have random dreams, dreams with missing gaps between scenes, or dreams that I couldn't remember when I woke up. After I expressed to her my frustration with this, the next morning after spending time in the secret place, I prayed that Holy Spirit would lead me to receiving and remembering dreams. I fell asleep and, as the dream started, I remember thinking to myself, "Now this is one coming in clear enough that I'll definitely remember it."

I dreamt that I was in a classroom setting and other guys were there in the desks around me. For some reason I knew that they were all husbands except for me. I was a "wife" but yet I looked the same, but I just knew I was a wife role (hang on, I know this already sounds weird.). The female teacher paused while teaching the class and said, "Miguel, this is for you." She had in her hand a letter that was folded up neatly. I knew I was opening this letter as being a "wife role" and found it to be a letter from my husband (Jesus) and the Father who I knew was simultaneously expressing His love for me here. Even from the onset of this dream it was a clear frequency in which I could remember and did not have gaps between scenes as with previous dreams.

I don't recall the wording of the letter but rather how it was making me feel; I was overwhelmed by His love and started to sob in tears. I then woke up and found myself smiling the biggest smile, knowing that my prayer had been divinely answered and that I had been drawn into this uniquely arranged dream. I felt that it was a way of him confirming that He had been drawing me into this realm more and that my eyes are going to be open more in my growing of His presence in understanding the spiritual realm. As for the inter- pretation? Well, even as I'm typing this, months after, I just received further elaboration from Holy Spirit than initially. Classrooms are where we are taught things intellectually for our mind (soul), which is all I had really experienced before, regarding the Scriptures and God Himself.

But as we've been learning throughout this book, God desires to take us deeper than that, so that we begin to live from our spirit (who is now one with His Spirit) and *then* have our mind and soul "renewed" to His new order, along with our body. In the dream, I was surrounded by "husbands" who only had an interest in intellectual, theological information for their brains, hence, why they were in the class. If you are acting the role of a husband, then you're the one leading the household and asking someone else to submit to your leading (you want a wife to come under *your* submission). This con- fusion of "roles" is what is at the core of religion – we try to submit God to our manmade shallow ways. We teach theologies and beliefs regarding the supernatural, "explaining" how He should operate or not, hence, us playing the husband role. But this is the very opposite position of what scripture teaches us we are to have. In scripture, Jesus is considered our "husband" and the church His bride.

Outside of the Biblical order, an *intimate* relationship with Jesus cannot be experienced. Instead we will end up settling for the applause and recognition of other religious "husbands" who have done the same mistake. But as we embrace our submissive "bride" role (wife), and honor Jesus as our husband and Lord of our household, we can receive all He has died to give us. We can experience the union Holy Spirit brings us into, so that just as Jesus and the Father are one so are we one with them. (Jn 17).

The teacher paused her instruction to give me the note, as if to say this note is more important for you to receive than my intellectual head-based instruction for these "husbands." As I unfolded the note, I was overcome by the deep expressions of intimacy from Jesus and the Father. Unfolding the note equals discovering the hidden or concealed matters of the Lord, namely what is in His heart.

From this day forward, I began to have many more dreams and visions along with my wife, and they continue to blow us away. For me, they come easier and clearer when I take a nap after I've just spent time in the secret place, rather than overnight, so I intentionally take a nap almost every time after the secret place. Some dreams and visions are just fun (flying experiences, humorous) others profound revelation, insight, instruction, while others are elaboration on something He taught me about Himself in the secret place that morning, and others even supernatural intercession for friends, family and strangers.

While the dreams prominently take place when I'm fully asleep, I've found that visions and actual spiritual encounters and supernatural intercession happen right when I'm just beginning to drift off in that half awake/half sleep state. It's all such a joy to explore because it's learning to hear our heavenly Dad's present voice and ways of His kingdom.

A great resource for understanding God's voice through dreams and visions is a book called, *The Divinity Code* by Adam F. Thompson and Adrian Beale. (I didn't say, *Divinci Code*. I said, "*DivINITY Code*.) Besides the main content of the book (which is really good and positively provoking) there are over four-hundred pages of a dream dictionary that gives hundreds and hundreds of biblical interpretation for different objects, scenarios, etc. that we may have dreamt. I also mentioned in a previous chapter, Brian Guerin's ministry, Bridal Glory (bridalglory.com) which also functions heavily in dreams, visions, prophetic, and has blessed me greatly too.

There have been several times while just drifting off to sleep, the Lord would supernaturally tune me into a particular scenario that needed immediate intercession – for complete strangers.

One recent example was I saw a dad (whom I didn't recognize as anyone I knew) sitting on a bed with his daughter (about age eight) with their backs against the headboard. His other daughter (about age four) was in the doorway of the room, and it looked like the three of them had just finished playing or something, because they were all smiling as if all was well. But then, the dad's face turned very serious as he told the four-year-old, "Okay it's time for Daddy to have adult time, close the door." As he said this, the four-year-old looked a little sad while the eight year old, who was sitting next to him on the bed became very nervous as if he had done this before. I immediately knew this was too specific to be a coincidence, especially since we rarely watched any T.V. and I couldn't remember the last secular movie or news we'd recently heard. So, I began to intercede for the girl since I knew in my spirit, she was a victim of sexual molestations from her dad, and this was about to be another time, repeating history, unless something supernatural took place.

> I interceded by commanding the angels of God to rush into the room and cast off every demonic presence. I prayed for the spirit of God to pierce through this man's heart, shaking him out of this moment and cycle, to see clearly the vulnerable child entrusted to his care by God. I prayed for God's tangible presence to bring the man into sobbing repentance and a new heart desiring healing for him and his daughters so that purity may be restored. I prayed the little girls would have their memories completely renewed into pureness and every trace of damage from this dysfunction to be eradicated in the name of Jesus.

When God clues us into a problem, or to a need for someone or a particular situation, it is always intentional and means He wants us to partner with Him in doing something about the situation to express His will into it. Just as Jesus modeled a Spirit-filled Son crushing the powers of darkness, so we are called into the very same lifestyle of Jesus to destroy the works of the devil. Which is why it is so imperative for us to know and follow His present voice and the present power of Holy Spirit.

As Joel 2 prophesied, "in the last days" these divine channels of communication will *intensify* not die off as religious circles claim. The more I experience these supernatural channels of God's voice, the more I see why the devil would want to keep us from experiencing God in these ways. It totally changes your appetite to want more encounters with God. It has always been God's idea to co-labor with us in regards to bringing lost children into His house, but His ways are only accessible through the Holy Spirit, and the Holy Spirit has only been given to us because of the cross of Christ, and the cross of Christ given to us because God the Father so loved the world that He sent His Son. Pray this prayer out loud with me:

> Father, I pray You supernaturally circumcise my heart from any and every trace of unbelief. Teach me how to simply receive You with childlike faith and expectancy. I want to become more aware and sensitive to Your present voice, in <u>all the ways</u> You desire to communicate with me today. Break off any religious chains and demonic strongholds that are currently keeping me from hearing Your voice more clearly, in Jesus' name, AMEN.

CHAPTER 10

SPIRITUAL SENSES RESTORED

We have talked a little about the new spirit we receive in our "new birth" and how that allows us to receive Holy Spirit to indwell inside of us. I also began to learn that our spirit, although physically not visible like flesh as our body is, it does have senses just like our body. Now I'm not trying to create a doctrine out of this, but rather share some provoking experiences and encounters in the spirit that will hopefully stir in you a greater faith and expectancy for more of the supernatural ways of God.

SPIRITUAL SMELLING/SCENT

One day I was listening to some testimonies from an older preacher named John G. Lake, while driving on the highway. The testimonies were so powerful that I literally began crying out, "Hallelujah. Oh, God, You're so good." I probably looked like a nut, but I was so overwhelmed with the presence of God that filled my car, as I was hearing about such testimony provoking me to a fresh revelation of who He is.

As the testimony finished, I thought to myself, "Man, we have no idea just how amazing He is and His ways are." Right after thinking this, I instantly smell a strong, concentrated, potent fragrance that I'd never smelled before. It was so sudden, it seemed like someone just sat down in my passenger seat saturated in the fragrance filling the entire car. It happened so suddenly and so strongly that I said out loud, "What is that? What is that?" And then I instantly heard, "Its heaven, its heaven."

Although my windows were closed, I looked around to see if maybe someone's car windows were down driving beside me, or if the smell was from something on the outside, but nothing in the natural could explain the origin of this smell. Nothing, other than a supernatural visit from either an angel or Jesus Himself who would carry heaven's fragrance. Perhaps such a visitation was affirmation of the powerful testimony I just heard as if to say, "Yup, you're hearing me now." My body, face, arms, and everything else, was tingling with hair standing up for the next several hours in response to that tangible presence from heaven. I had never smelled anything like that before. Weeks after, while looking into various scents, oils, and fragrances trying to find a comparison, the closest thing I found to be what I smelled, was a mixture of frankincense and myrrh. The very two fragrances the wise men brought baby Jesus in the manger.

Since that time, I feel like Holy Spirit will occasionally open up my spiritual sense of smell to tune me in to the angelic or even demonic realm that may be in process of doing something in or near the person in front of me or around me. When it has been a demonic presence nearby, I've smelled a strong stench of excrement and garbage waste combined (while no garbage, garbage truck, waste field, or sewer nearby). There was even a time that I experienced a supernatural heightening of smell when driving in a distant vicinity of a liquor store and smelling a strong sense of alcohol, as if someone had just opened up a bottle of tequila in my car with the windows closed.

Just as we are able to associate certain colognes and perfumes with certain people who've just left an elevator or room, so in the spiritual realm, God wants to tune our sense of smell in the spirit man, to detect the presence of light and darkness.

I know these testimonies could sound far out to some who are reading now, however I hope instead of taking an offense to them, you instead, ask the Lord to quicken your spiritual scent and watch what He begins to do through that.

SPIRITUAL HEARING

There are times when God speaks to my spirit and moves my heart to share a very specific thought or word for a stranger or loved one. The accuracy of it would touch them so profoundly that they knew it was directly supernatural from God. Sometimes, it's just one word highlighting a body part that the person needs healing in, or other times it may be a quick image or vision of a situation that person is struggling with (The Bible refers to this as "a word of knowledge" in 1 Cor.12:8).

As I'm growing, I'm learning it is a process or training from Holy Spirit, but always from a place of love. In my growing, I may miss it or mistake hearing something but since my approach was genuinely out of God's love for the person, love never fails and they never mock or think I'm dumb for reaching out to them. Instead, they really appreciate the act of love and the fact I would even step out for them. I believe as we become more in tune with our spirit and Holy Spirit's activity speaking to us there, this will be more and more a part of the believer's everyday life.

The Bible refers to God's voice as a "still small voice" or a "gentle whisper" in 1 Kings 19:12. What has blown me away about learning how to tune into His voice, is how long I had mistaken His voice as my own thoughts. I always thought that if I was going to start hearing from God, I'd hear Him audibly in my natural ears or in such a loud internal voice unlike anything I'd heard before. And while it is possible to hear Him in such ways at times, more than likely you have already been hearing Him speaking to you your whole life, but perhaps haven't learned how to discern His voice from your own thoughts.

Our thoughts come from our mind, but He speaks to us through our spirit which feels like a deeper place in our heart. Hence, why it becomes easier to discern His voice as our spirit is maturing. But the maturity of our spirit isn't what has qualified us to have Him speak to us but it allows us to tune into the frequency He has always spoken to us through. I love this because it shows He hasn't been some Father who stayed silent until we met a certain level of holiness first, but instead a Father who has always been very active in speaking to His children. I love learning how to hear His voice.

I hear Him elaborate on a scripture I've just read by bringing it to life; I love hearing Him tell me *specific* things related to a situation I'm facing, insight into someone else's situation (health issue, recent tragedy) that will allow me to express His specific intention and love for them, His thoughts of me, and much more. God's written Word gets "breathed on" in a life giving, practical way, if we'd tune into His present speaking. It takes what God once said and translates it into what He is saying to us specifically. One doesn't contradict the other, but instead drives it deeper into our practical lives. Religion operates in the past, speaking of God, but is void of His present speaking and voice, and therefore limits us to a surface experience of the gospel, as it keeps it in the distance of mere doctrine apart from living transformation. Jesus said in Jn 6:63, "the words that I speak unto you, they are spirit, and they are life." This was in the context of speaking to the religious leaders who believed in the *past* speaking of God through Moses but not the *present* speaking of God through Jesus (see previous verses). God's written Word (Bible) apart from His presence and present speaking of Holy Spirit, is misinterpreted, misapplied, and misunderstood, as it will only be viewed from the human intellect and mind just as the Pharisees of Jesus time had done. However, the Bible is only unveiled by the same Spirit of God who breathed it into the hearts of the men who wrote it.

He is the one who imparts to us the "words Jesus **is** speaking to us" and therefore, feeding our spirit man (not mere intellect) as His present speaking is "spirit and life" to us. God's written word and present speaking have the same intention, namely, to impart the living Christ into our spirit by the Holy Spirit, as His presence is the only source which abundant life flows from.

There have been times where His voice literally wakes me up as if I'm tuning into Him mid-sentence, and after I write down what I heard, it's the most profound revelation that my own thoughts would have never been able to muster. For example, He once woke me up saying, "Divine life is made manifest when man ceases so that My Spirit may flow effortlessly through him." I loved it.

One early morning, after I had spent some alone time, worshipping in an empty church, I sat down in a recliner to take a nap. After falling into a deep sleep, I heard a man talking to someone else as clear as day, as though he was literally standing right in front of me. It was so real that it woke me up. But I thought it was just the man I was expecting to meet up with soon, and that he had walked up to where I was resting while still talking to someone who was with him. It sounded so loud and close as if two men were literally standing arm's length away from me. But as my mind started to process what I was hearing, and my eyes were about to open to see who was here in front of me talking, it instantly stopped mid-sentence, and I soon realized there was still nobody else physically present in the entire building. I heard Holy Spirit tell me, "That was your angel talking to another angel while you were resting, but when he noticed you were actually beginning to hear him and wake up to his voice, he stopped talking." All I could do was laugh. God is much more fun that what many of us make Him out to be. He loves surpassing our expectations and stirring a childlike faith and expectancy in us by doing things like this. We often think if it isn't extremely deep or vitally important than God isn't interested in doing it but I find that isn't true. He's so in love with us that He uses even the simplest things to shower us with perspective changing love.

SPIRITUAL SEEING/SIGHT

I've had experiences where I begin to see a light (while my eyes are closed) but as it would get brighter it felt so real that I'd physically open my eyes to see it, only to realize it wasn't coming from the natural realm. I did this mistake so many times at first, because I didn't realize He was trying to show me how to allow my "spiritual eyes" to see instead of my physical, hence, why it would instantly stop when I opened my physical eyes or continue to get brighter if I kept those eyes intentionally shut and yield to what I was "seeing" internally.

Some people are able to see with their "spiritual eyes" while wide awake or for a brief moment that the Holy Spirit tunes them in. I've only had a few experiences like this so far. But other times your body and physical eyes may have to be at rest to allow your spirit and spiritual eyes the opportunity to "see" without getting interrupted in the natural.

One time, after praying, I started to get sleepy and closed my eyes for a quick nap. I saw myself walking through an empty office setting and Jesus was walking toward me. At first, I said, "Wait, is this Jesus coming toward me?" And then as He was a foot or so away, I realized it was. Just as He took another two steps right into me, I was instantly filled with an overwhelming tangible presence that woke me up and continued to linger on my entire body while I was awake laying there, for another minute or so. It felt like when your leg falls asleep and you're hitting it and feel those pins and needles feeling, except imagine it ten times more powerful and over and in every cell of your body all at once.

I had felt that once before that experience, in a dream where He had woken me up similarly. I felt like something had been awakened in my spirit from that time forward, because I began to physically feel God's presence in that manner more, in addition to other ways He had previously manifested His presence. Sometimes a new encounter or experience is actually an impartation for us to start experiencing God's presence in that particular way from that point forward.

SPIRITUAL FEELING/TOUCH

Another day, after spending time in the secret place, I laid down for a nap while praying that Holy Spirit would lead me into an encounter. It felt as if immediately after closing my eyes, I was suddenly kneeling down. I then felt the presence of someone coming near to me from behind, while His left hand gently rested on my left shoulder. I instantly knew in my spirit it was a male figure and that it was Jesus. At first it was such a tangible, sudden touch that it really startled me and humanly I wanted to open my eyes to look behind me to see if someone had broken in our house or something and was behind me doing this. But those concerns were quickly subdued as when He touched me, I begin to feel His power and presence overwhelm me to tears and my body was trembling, not being able to withstand the power coming from him into my body. I remember kneeling there and receiving this while saying something along the lines of "I want more of you, Jesus," until it eventually stopped. I then opened my eyes and realized my body had been laying down the whole time.

Now, I know that may stretch some reading this right now, but this is so elementary in comparison to Philip in the Bible, who teleported thirty miles away, not just in spirit, but with his entire body, soul, and spirit. (ACTS 8:26-40). In that story, he has an angel show up and give him direct instructions, then the Holy Spirit tells him further instructions, and once he completed the instructions (sharing the gospel with somebody), Holy Spirit instantly whisked his entire body, soul, and spirit away to a whole other town. It's a good thing Philip believed and was tuned into such supernatural communications from heaven. Someone else's salvation depended on it that day.

There have been several times when I was about to get up from my bed, and suddenly felt the mattress and sheets move from the foot of the bed like when somebody sits at the foot of the bed and then gets off. I thought for sure it was my wife getting out of bed or climbing in, but when I opened my eyes there was nobody in or near the bed. I thought, "could it be an angel?" This happened several times, to the point where, one morning, I told God, "Lord, I really don't want to be assuming things to be supernatural if perhaps it's something else naturally explainable, so please give me a confirmation this is truly supernatural." Just a couple of hours later, my wife who I had *not* shared those things with yet, told me, "The craziest thing happened this morning while you were in the secret place. I felt like someone was getting off the bed from sitting on it as the sheet moved but then I opened my eyes and you weren't here." I laughed and then shared with her the same thing that had been happening to me and how I just prayed for confirmation. We gratefully thanked God for confirming this supernatural activity.

One time while driving and listening to a powerful sermon, I was so touched, I remember feeling like I was literally erupting from deep within as I was so moved by His Spirit. I immediately felt the urgency to worship Him out loud in my car yelling, "Yes, Jesus. Hallelujah. You're so worthy, Lord." I suddenly felt a buzz-like feeling come over my entire body, and an incredible joy. I parked to go into a store, but when I stepped out of my car, I could barely keep my balance. I thought, "What in the world?" I felt like I was high or something but on the Holy Spirit. This high lasted for the next fifteen minutes as I wandered through Walmart, smiling ear to ear, blissed out in the presence of God.

I know that could sound weird, especially since our culture is much more familiar with the counterfeit "high" from drugs. But remember, Satan can only counterfeit things that originated from God. We give him too much credit sometimes and we're quick to label and shun such experiences out of fearing the counterfeit. God's presence can be tangibly felt like this or even as heat over a particular body part, your head, even your whole body. Oftentimes when praying for a healing for someone, they will describe feeling heat in the body part that needs healing, and sure enough they would be completely healed instantly or shortly after. ("God is a consuming fire"-Heb.12:29) Some people experience tingling, electricity like power or none of those, but yet fully healed after the prayer. Those same manifestations of Holy Spirit's presence can also be experienced in corporate service settings, in the Secret Place, while adoring Him in worship, and even throughout your day. Remember He is IN YOU..

Hebrews 5:14 says, "But solid food is for the *mature*, who because of practice have their *senses trained* to discern good and evil."

Sometimes we are so skeptical, that we have more faith in what taking an aspirin would do to our physical body than the tangible presence of a supernatural God living inside of us. Just a "feeling" of His presence isn't what we are after. We are after Him. Feelings won't always be there even though He is always present. But feeling His tangible presence feels as comforting and real as a husband and wife feel when close to one another. It's not the only substance of their relationship, but not having it enough or at all would show there's serious dysfunction.

The reality is much of the body of Christ (the church) has become numb to His presence for fear of falling into emotionalism or fanaticism, but again, that is just as unhealthy as a married couple who doesn't express any physical touching toward one another, and it affects our relationship with God very similarly. That's all I knew for most of my life and all I believed was available to us. But the more things I've experienced in the secret place and in corporate settings the more humbled I've become to receiving how practical and visible a touch from God can look like. I'm not as quick to label, judge, and criticize as I used to be, because I've personally seen and also witnessed in others, that when a physical manifestation is truly from God touching that person, true change and transformation is sure to follow in that person's life. Even if the manifestation looked weird, made me uncomfortable (like many have) I knew the fruit would testify of exactly *whom* had touched that person's life at the moment. What if we tested all manifestations and fruit like this before being so quick to say, "It's the devil." Don't merely judge from what is seen in the visible physical manifestation, as I can tell you firsthand, when God touches people, it can manifest in something as simple as tears overwhelming a person to as crazy as a person getting thrown to the ground, from over five feet. Seriously. But test what follows, and if it's of the devil, all that emotional, crazy looking, falling over, dramatic expression will be nothing more than that. But if it's of God, significant breakthrough, deliverance of demons, healings, and restoration are sure to be the fruit of what appeared to be just crazy on the outside.

I invite you to start paying more attention from this point forward to what you're sensing in your heart and feeling even tangibly on your body, face, etc. when worshiping, praying, and even during this prayer. I know it's the will of our heavenly Father that every one of our cells is awakened to just how near and close to us He really is.

> *Father, I pray you quicken all my senses, to be used for Your glory, and for the kingdom's causes. I dedicate my sense of smell, touch, hearing, seeing, and taste to You, that they may be sanctified, set apart, and tuned into what You are doing and saying, so that I may become a better receiver of Your presence. Just as my physical senses are tuned into this natural physical realm, I pray my spiritual senses be tuned into Your supernatural spiritual realm, in Jesus' name, Amen.*

CHAPTER 11

SPIRITUAL REALITIES BYPASSING PHYSICAL LAWS

In Acts Chapter 8, there's a story of a man named Philip, who gets a message from an angel, instructing him to go down a specific road. He went to the road he was instructed to go down and found an Ethiopian man in a chariot, reading the Scriptures, specifically the part in Isaiah that speaks of Jesus. Then the Holy Spirit told Philip to join him in his chariot (Acts 8:29). It was vitally important for Philip to be aware and expectant of God's messages through divine angels and the voice of the Holy Spirit. There are such amazing exploits and adventures awaiting God's children, if we'd just tune in to the *present* activity and *speaking* of heaven. In Philip's case, this divine appointment allowed him to explain the Scriptures to the man, leading him to Christ and baptizing him. It's obvious that Philip understood and believed in the Scriptures (written Word of God) but he was also very aware and in tune with God's present ability to speak to us through supernatural revelation, instruction, and visitation as God did through an angel and through His Spirit in this story. But the story doesn't stop there. Listen to what verses 39-40 of Acts 8 says:

> [39] When they came up out of the water, the Spirit of the Lord snatched Philip away; and the eunuch no longer saw him, but went on his way rejoicing. [40] But Philip found himself at Azotus, and as he passed through he kept preaching the gospel to all the cities until he came to Caesarea."

Did you catch that? In an instant, he was completely (body, soul, and spirit), supernaturally teleported to Azotus, which was approximately over thirty miles away. This story shows just how specific, intentional, and limitless our heavenly Father is to express His love and care to His children. This story isn't just recording the salvation of this Ethiopian, which is amazing in itself, but it is also giving us a provoking example of how supernatural God's ways and voice truly are. There are so many testimonies in the book of Acts, displaying the supernatural fruit that God wants to produce through our lives as evidence of His living presence. He is the living God, not a statue or monument we worship and talk about.

Ezekiel wasn't even in the era of the New Covenant and yet had a similar experience:

> "Then I looked, and behold, a likeness as the appearance of a man; from His loins and downward there was the appearance of fire, and from His loins and upward the appearance of brightness, like the appearance of glowing metal. 3He stretched out the form of a hand *and caught me by a lock of my head; and the Spirit lifted me up between earth and heaven* and brought me in the visions of God to Jerusalem, to the entrance of the north gate of the inner court, where the seat of the idol of jealousy, which provokes to jealousy, was located. 4And behold, the glory of the God of Israel was there, like the appearance which I saw in the plain." Ezekiel 8:2-4.

How incredible. This took place *prior* to the completed work of the Cross which means even this experience was *inferior* to what you and I can access in the Spirit today.

Paul said, in 2 Corinthians 12:2-4, "I know a man in Christ who fourteen years ago—whether in the body I do not know, or *out of the body* I do not know, God knows—such a man was caught up to the third heaven. 3 And I know how such a man—whether *in the body or apart from the body* I do not know, God knows— 4 was caught up into Paradise and heard inexpressible words, which a man is not permitted to speak."

113

Regardless of our modern man-made, religious rationales and limitations, there is a reality *apart from the body*, according to the Bible. The devil has done much to distort such things with the new age movement, but please note the spiritual realities apart from the body originated from God, not the Devil. Such experiences are usually shunned from being discussed in religious circles since it doesn't fit into the "measured out" predictable confines of religion. But what if that's exactly what the Devil wants? If what the Bible says is true regarding spirit travel and re-location, then there is a dimension of supernatural realities and possibilities we have handed over for the Devil to utilize for his benefit rather than for the kingdom of heaven as it was intended.

The famous verse, John 3:16, isn't about just a mental acknowledgement of "God so loved the world that He gave His son..."

Believing in Him isn't just saying, "I believe He died for my sins..." But it's also believing the spiritual realities He died to give us – the eternal/spiritual life. It's believing we aren't slaves to sin and the old, limited, physical realm as we all were prior to Jesus death. It's believing we are *now* God's own sons/daughters, made "new creations/creatures (2 Cor.5:17) for spirit-to-Spirit union with God once again. After hearing the Gospel, we have no excuse to continue living with the same physical limitations as we did prior to believing. Yet so many Christians who proclaim they *believe* reject the full realities and gift of the supernatural, spiritual life that has been redeemed.

I know, because I was one of them for most of my life in the church and as a minister of the Gospel. I believe it's the devil's goal to keep us handicapped from our true supernatural identities and abilities as spiritual beings, so that we'd neglect what we have access to now. The weekly religious activities and traditions that most of us have grown up with, have become the means of our "born again" identities, rather than the supernatural indwelling and union of our spirit and God's spirit. Those activities and beliefs are a false security that we point to when we doubt our spiritual maturity, but they fall so short of the New Testament realities of God's spiritual realm we are called to rule over as co-heirs with Jesus.

I've seen the huge difference in my life the more I've learned my identity as a spiritual being/son of a God, and actually believed and embraced what the Gospel says about my new identity in Christ. As my secret place time continued to grow and my spirit became more aware of His presence, I began to have some interesting experiences that have now evolved into similar experiences, as mentioned in the above texts.

Almost every one of these experiences happened as I was about to nap after spending my time in the secret place. For me, I find my spirit to be most receptive to God's Spiritual dreams, visions, and encounters after it has been refreshed and tuned in during the secret place time.

As I shared in previous chapters, I began to get spiritual dreams which eventually led to visions. But then something else started to happen. The Holy Spirit began to train me on how to let Him lead me by my spirit instead of my head/mind getting in the way. For example, (I mentioned in a previous chapter) as I'd begin to drift off into my nap, I'd see a small, very bright light that was getting brighter. My mind would then kick in and say, "Open your eyes to see it." But when I'd open my physical eyes, everything would stop. I began to realize that this light wasn't from the natural realm, but the spiritual realm, hence, why when I'd try to use my physical/natural eyes I'd come out of it.

Little by little as these experiences would happen, it became easier to let my spiritual eyes continue to see and my natural eyes to rest. I soon realized that my spiritual eyes were just part of this training. God wanted me to learn how to tune into all my spiritual senses that my spirit man has. His realm is spiritual, after all, "God is spirit" (Jn 4), so the more open we are to letting Him reveal Himself to us the more of His realm becomes the reality we are most aware of.

As mentioned in the story of Philip, New Testament believers were very aware of their inheritance and access to the things of God, hence, the plethora of testimonies displaying the supernatural. I've been extremely skeptical of such encounters and experiences because of all the fear driven statements I've read and taught my whole religious life. But God meets us where we are and patiently and lovingly reveals Himself one revelation at a time, at a pace that is sensitive to our willingness to learn. These "look into the light" experiences began to cause my spirit man to be more active and my body/mind more surrendered. I felt like God was trying to encourage my spirit man to believe and act beyond the physical limitations of my body. I had several experiences where I was out of my physical body and ascending toward the ceiling of my bedroom, but then my mind would interrupt once again and get me out of it as my trying to make sense of what was happening. Eventually, I allowed it to happen longer and for further "distances" up and around which felt incredible. Then it advanced to the following kind of experiences:

One time, in the morning (after just spending several hours in the secret place), around the time kids would be riding the bus to school, I had just drifted off to sleep and instantly found myself standing on the back bumper of a school bus, looking in, seeing it filled with high school students. I knew they couldn't see me, but that God totally knew who they each were. Throughout this experience, I heard a whirlwind-like sound in the background. I've noticed this same sound with several other experiences where I felt I had traveled in the spirit somewhere. As I stood on the back bumper, I felt so filled with the presence and power of God. I could feel His presence radiating off of me and I felt this bold confidence, knowing He was about to do something great here. I had an internal confidence from my spirit that knew I was literally standing there at the moment. It all just seemed to make so much sense to me, as if I had gone on many spirit travel missions before although I hadn't. Since I knew I was in the spirit, I didn't open the back door, but instead walked right through it. As I walked down the middle aisle, I waited for the place God would prompt me to sit. I then saw these two high school boys laughing and, from the looks on their faces and in their eyes, I knew they were high on some type of substance.

I heard one say to the other, "Man, I just love how drugs makes me feel." I sat right in the middle of them and, with my left hand, I cupped the chin and cheeks of the boy on the left then with my right hand the chin and cheeks of the boy on my right and just said, "Jesus…" I felt God's power coming out from me into both of them and they both said, "Whoa…" I could feel them both trembling as the power of God was delivering them from their addictions. Yet, they were left in such relief. It was absolutely an incredible thing to witness. I then could hear me back in my room as I opened my eyes. I felt like when you've woken up from a very deep sleep and don't know where you are or what time it is.

Another time, while just drifting off to sleep, I felt as if I had entered into a hospital room in my spirit. I had heard a guy's first and last name from God, then found it on the doorway, and knew the one who I was walking up to in bed was him. He was an elderly white gentleman, who was skinny with a small, distended belly, and he was moaning in pain.

I could hear him say, "Oh, God, please help me, I'm in so much pain..." And so, I walked up closer, and put my hand over his stomach torso area, and my other hand on his head. I turned my affections in towards God and felt overwhelmed by an overflow of the Holy Spirit's power and presence. I then told all the pain to leave and said to the man, "Be filled with Holy Spirit and receive complete healing in Jesus' name." I then looked at his face and his countenance change, as if receiving great relief. He then said, "Oh, thank you, God." I saw nurses walking in the hallway and they looked toward him as if wondering what was going on with him.

I remember wondering, "can they see me?" One of them walked in to ask the man how he was doing and he said, "Fine." She then peeked at his IV bags and left. I thought, "I'd better look more engaged with him before they think I'm some creeper" (since he didn't even know me.) At that point, I felt like I was in my body or at least able to be seen, and I began to ask him how he was doing.

He said "Good."

As the nurse walked in, I said something to him about God, "I see God is blessing you, huh?"

Then he said, "Ah, see, why do you have to bring that up?" He slowly got up out of bed and walked over to the other, empty bed.

I said, "Because He's the one that is healing you."

He responded, "Well, I don't believe in Him or any of that stuff." At that point, his face wasn't the old man, but it was of an atheist friend I knew (as though God was highlighting to me he was an atheist).

I said, "Well, you will. I'm praying right now you encounter His touch in such a profound way you cannot deny it was supernaturally Him. Be filled with the Spirit of God, in Jesus' name." I know I said more things but I can't remember, but as I was praying, I could hear the nurse who had sat down in the chair by the adjacent wall saying, "Yes, Jesus, amen."

After I said *amen*, I smiled to her and she had tears in her eyes. I said, "His presence is so good right?" I then turned to him and said, "That peace you're feeling is Him. He's here." I asked the nurse if she had anything she needed or wanted prayer for. She said, "More of His presence." So, I grabbed her hand and began to pray. She became overwhelmed with the Holy Spirit, she had tears running down her face and began to tremble. I then came out of the experience.

I've had other similar experiences. Even one was where I was waking up in China and being taken toward the underground church. I long to have many more such experiences.

I've heard of many other testimonies like this from other believers too and it's so provoking to hear of. But I believe this is still barely scratching the surface of what God is inviting us to experience in the power of His Spirit and His kingdom realm.

In Acts 2:22, just after the outpouring of the Holy Spirit, Peter is preaching under the power of the Holy Spirit and says this,

> "Jesus the Nazarene, a man attested to you *(Greek=shown, displayed, exhibited to you)* by God with miracles and wonders and signs which God performed through Him in your midst, just as you yourselves know..."

Notice how God "attested/displayed" endorsement to "Jesus the Nazarene," "with miracles, wonders, and signs, which God performed through Him in your midst...."

Then you read the rest of Acts and see how just as Jesus was endorsed by those things, so did the apostles have signs, wonders, miracles "follow" them wherever they went. *Nowhere in Scripture will you find God saying that one day in the future or in the last days He will no longer endorse His true disciples this way.* Nowhere in Scripture do you find instructions telling us to stop expecting Him to move and speak the way we read He did in Scripture. There are many modern-day theologians, pastors, and false prophets who have come up with all kinds of doctrine, theology, and explanations to defend the lack of supernatural fruit in their own lives, and there are many men and women who will choose to embrace such false security in those "explanations" to exempt themselves from a deeper examination of their personal experience with Jesus today and their actual spiritual bankruptcy. But the world is groaning to see the sons and daughters of God *manifested* and *demonstrating* their supernatural identities, as these demonstrations reflect the *living presence and voice of the living God,* who is our Father. It's impossible to claim to be co-laboring with the living Christ and not have *the way* He ministered flowing through us. Jesus wasn't sent to merely pass on a set of theological doctrine, but instead He imparted the very presence of God Himself back into the spirit/heart of man.

The religious culture I came from shunned the present speaking and miraculous encounters with the living God. In fact, there was so much focus and emphasis on the devil as the big deceiver in these last days, that any and every testimony I heard regarding a healing today, or supernatural encounter I quickly labeled as the enemy's deception. *But through such heightened skepticism, I had developed a greater faith in the devil's ability to deceive than God's ability to save and deliver in the present.* The result? I had the same lack of fruit of the miraculous, encounters, and adventures with Holy Spirit, that my leadership did, accompanied with the same unbelief they'd developed. However, God's tolerance with such stale, powerless, religiosity is crushed with the true Gospel and presence of the living God.

The supernatural realm of God is intimidating and even uncomfortable at times, as it challenges everything in our natural and physical upbringing and experience of life thus far. However, speaking of the Holy Spirit Jesus says in Jn. 14:16,

> [16] And I will pray the Father, and he shall give you another Comforter, that he may abide with you forever;

Pray this prayer out loud:

> *Father, I surrender to the fact that my understanding is inferior to the spiritual realities You dwell in. I desire to be a heart, body, mind, and spirit that You desire to dwell in and express Yourself through. I desire to have childlike faith in Your abilities to defy the natural laws and limitations of the world. I want to experience the adventures You have long desired for me to experience. Break my walls down so that you can have **all** of me, in Jesus' name, Amen.*

CHAPTER 12

PURE FOLLOWERS OF THE LAMB

> "These are the ones who were not defiled with women,
> for they are virgins. These are the ones who follow
> the Lamb wherever He goes." Revelation 14:4 NKJV.

If you read the context of this verse, it is speaking of the last day remnant people of God that are on earth right before the Lord returns. "Not defiled with women for they are virgins" isn't referring to the natural realm (all married men would be excluded.), but instead a spiritual setting of oneself aside *wholly* for the bridegroom, Jesus. It means no dabbling into relationships with other women, or things that would draw our affections away from the one who has given Himself entirely and exclusively to us.

It then says, "These are the ones who follow the Lamb (Jesus) wherever He goes (or "is going")." I believe the *virgin* kind of devotion to the Lord referred to here is our living reality *naturally*, *as* our following of the Lamb becomes more intimate, and our proximity to Him is nearer and nearer. But what does "following the Lamb wherever He goes" really mean and look like?

Some churches say it's adhering to a particular set of doctrines and guarding them closely. But Jesus says, in John 10:27 NKJV, "²⁷ *My sheep hear My voice*, and *I know them*, and *they follow Me*." As someone once said, "Jesus didn't say my sheep know my book but my sheep hear my voice and I know them..." As we've discussed in this first half of the book, "hearing His voice" is imperative to the believer if we are to truly be *His follower*. You can be a "follower" of many other things, people, ministries, and denominations now a days and still not be following the *living* Christ. When we don't hear or understand the ways He speaks, we place the living God into the same inactivity and inattentiveness as a monument statue in a museum.

Museums contain the memories and statues of "great things or people" accompanied by written words describing the history and facts about them. However, they are dead and lifeless, no *living voice*, conversation, or fellowship. God's written Word is not a mere written description of a lifeless, inactive, God. It isn't merely a collection of historical data describing the Christ who *once* was alive doing the works of the Father, but instead the Christ who IS alive presently doing the works of the Father just as He did before. In understanding His voice, we enter a practical, vibrant, real, experience with Him that surpasses any worldly pleasure that the devil tries to give us in exchange. The word Jesus uses for "know" in the text above in Jn. 10:27, is not head knowledge, but actual "experientially knowing" which goes beyond a book and into the very heart, Spirit to spirit, communion with the living God.

When Jesus was here on earth in bodily form, He was the living, active, presence of the living God on earth. But when He left, the Father could then send us the most precious gift – His very own Spirit, which is *presently* the current, active, presence of the living God. Holy Spirit is the interactive presence of the living God that draws us into the realities of our redeemed status and privileges. If you remove Him from the picture, we are left with a hollow shell of religious ideas and theories without any tangible *power* or *presence* of the living God.

If there is any deception that should be of highest priority to be aware of is that "in these last days...there will be a *form* of godliness, but denying its power." -2 Timothy 3:1,5. Lifeless, powerless religion is not merely a watered down version of God's truth but a direct opposition to the gospel. "For I am not ashamed of the gospel of Jesus Christ for it is the *power of God unto salvation....*" -Romans 1:16. Powerless, presence-less religion and form is not okay. No matter how popular, how common, how long we've seen it, been in it, and lived with it. God clearly gives us the blueprint for following Jesus and it is through hearing His voice through the various ways He speaks to us. His present voice speaks into even the smallest details of our day to day lives and draws us deeper into the realities of heaven on earth.

Our spirit and Holy Spirit can mature in relational depth together, and overflow from within us out onto our external reality. Jesus tells us what kind of fruit would spontaneously follow out of such intimacy and believing in Him, "casting out demons, healing the sick, raising the dead." (Mk.16:17-18; Matthew 10:1). These are the very things it is impossible for us to do without His supernatural Spirit and presence. It is no coincidence Jesus would place such a description as it requires the *present speaking* of God's voice and the *tangible presence* of His Spirit in intimate relationship with us to fulfill. What's amazing to me is the more I grow in my intimacy with Jesus (Spirit to spirit), the more clearly I see how paralyzing the many forms of human religion have masqueraded as the genuine spiritual experience. It's as if we've become so numb to His clear statements of truth on this subject, and it's glossed over as if simply "not applicable for today."

"The doctrine stating, 'Signs and wonders are no longer needed because we have the Bible' was created by people who hadn't seen God's power and needed an explanation to justify their own powerless churches." -*When heaven invades earth*, by Bill Johnson. The man, Bill Johnson, who wrote that, is an individual whose life and ministry is marked with many healings, miracles, and sound biblical teaching. Much of his ministry is tracked on *Bethel.tv* and has been one of the many ministries the Lord led me to regarding present day followers of His presence. There are countless pages of doctor-confirmed healings along with an explosive amount of disciples of Jesus who've been launched out from that ministry. Bill Johnson has numerous books and sermons that have blessed me and been very affirming to what Holy Spirit has been leading us through. But even that ministry is just one of the abundant areas and places where God's tangible presence and fruit is being demonstrated on the earth right now. Another great book is, *There is More* by Dr. Randy Clark. He also has many books and resources regarding healing for today, modern revival, and so much more. His life and ministry *globalawakening.com* are also marked with many supernatural fruits and insights to the present day moving of God. What I love about each place or ministry the Holy Spirit has led us to glean from, is at the core of everything they teach, is intimacy with Jesus. There's a constant focus of hearing the voice of God for today, and equipping believers to more fully receive and believe the Gospel of Jesus Christ in their practical lifestyle rather than a mere external theology.

There is only one unpardonable sin, not two or three but one: blaspheming the Holy Spirit, Mark 3:29. Why? Because His presence is what joins our spirit with His and brings us back into *practical union* with our heavenly Father, who "is spirit." (Jn. 4) The Gospel isn't a mere positional change to be experienced once in heaven. It's the practical rejoining, redeeming, of God and man now through Holy Spirit to human spirit communion. No matter how many scriptures we memorize, how many commandments we pride ourselves in keeping, when we blaspheme the *present* working of God by His supernatural Spirit, we alienate ourselves from the practical experience of the Gospel and settle for a lifeless form. Not only that, but we come into agreement with the anti-Christ (anti-anointing) spirit. It is not uncommon to go to any nearby church and hear about the works and ministry of God the Father and the works and ministry of Jesus Christ. Thousands upon thousands of Christians week after week recount the works of them both, while ignoring the present presence of God, the Holy Spirit, who is longing for a people who will exchange their worship of form for His tangible supernatural presence. It isn't hard to find a church who can tell us about the Gospel of Jesus while never introducing us or teaching us how to engage with the Holy Spirit whom Jesus died to send to us. The Gospel is robbed of its true power when told merely as a past story. God has given us His tangible presence as the living reality of the Gospel of Jesus rather than just a great theory *one day to be experienced.*

It is impossible to truly co-labor with Jesus without a lifestyle that looks just like His. Nowhere in Scripture does it say the life of Jesus and the early church was a demonstration that would only be *temporarily* applicable for the apostolic era only. That is a demonic rationalization that blasphemes the living presence and voice of God. Look how the Bible emphasizes the supernatural endorsement of God through signs, wonders, and miracles, and how His voice and demonstrative presence were released *simultaneously* together.

> "And Jesus went about all Galilee, teaching in their synagogues, preaching the gospel of the kingdom, and healing all kinds of sickness and all kinds of disease among the people." Mat 4:23 NKJV.

> "Then Jesus went about all the cities and villages, teaching in their synagogues, preaching the gospel of the kingdom, and healing every sickness and every disease among the people." Matthew 9:35 NKJV.

> "And as you go, preach, saying, 'The kingdom of heaven is at hand.' Heal the sick, cleanse the lepers, raise the dead, cast out demons. Freely you have received, freely give." Matthew 10:7-8 NKJV.

"And heal the sick there, and say to them, 'The kingdom of God has come near to you." Lk 10:9 NKJV. Notice how Jesus defines the kingdom of God as coming near a person: when the sick is healed. He mentions other supernatural deliverances of demons, raising the dead, etc. in other verses, all pointing to the fact that His intention is to release the *present reality* of His kingdom here "on earth as it is in heaven." Practical demonstrations of the living, supernatural God and nothing less. No lifeless, powerless, words; just raw demonstrations of God's power conquering sin, disease, and affliction.

> Do you not believe that I am in the Father, and the Father in Me? The words that I speak to you I do not speak on My own *authority;* but the Father who dwells in Me does the works. John 14:10 NKJV.

> As You sent Me into the world, I also have sent them into the world. John 17:8 NKJV.

> Heaven's mandate for the follower of Jesus is exactly that – following Jesus. Satan is very quick to offer an alternative to a person, even in the very *form* of religious garb, but it is an obvious elephant in the room when contrasted against the living Christ and the living Gospel of love and supernatural power.

[29] Now, Lord, look on their threats, and grant to Your servants that with all boldness they may speak Your word,[30] by stretching out Your hand to heal, and that signs and wonders may be done through the name of Your holy Servant Jesus. [31] And when they had prayed, the

place where they were assembled together was shaken; and they were all filled with the Holy Spirit, and they spoke the word of God with boldness. Acts 4:29-31 NKJV.

> Notice what Peter describes is "speaking God's word," healings, signs, and wonders done in the name of Jesus. Notice the tangible evidence manifested when Holy Spirit came, "The place where they were assembled together was *shaken*." God is still the same interactive God. He has not changed His mind as far as the degree of interactive activity He desires to have with us. But we alienate ourselves from His activity when we exchange His living truth for crippling lies.

"in mighty signs and wonders, by the power of the Spirit of God, so that from Jerusalem and round about to Illyricum I have *fully preached the gospel of Christ*." Romans 15:19 NKJV. A gospel message that is merely, in word, is an incomplete Gospel and will produce fruit bearing the same lack. People come into church diseased, sick, afflicted and leave the exact same way *if* all we have to offer is a "kind word of encouragement" or "hope for a future God who will come back to deliver them." But a complete Gospel, fully preached, is one accompanied by a living *demonstration* of "mighty signs and wonders by the power of the living Spirit of God."

I'm so thankful that God is far from being asleep. His presence is so fun to track all over the globe in the numerous and various areas, ministries, people, and countries where the living God is still present to heal, deliver, and even resurrect. I cannot keep up with all that He is doing. It's becoming the new normal and it should be since He's the one who said, "the kingdom of heaven is at hand."

It has become so common in today's culture to learn the proper cliché phrases of Christianity such as, "I've been born again, filled with the Holy Spirit, follower of Jesus," while remaining absent of His tangible presence and fruit, and having no problem with it. There is such a false security in the religious blueprints, that one finds no reason or hunger to truly seek the Lord's heart on these fundamental truths of the Gospel. We'd rather say, "Well, here God I'll give you this instead," whether that be our commitment to attend church once a week, pay tithe, or whatever. All great things, but secondary to the priorities of Heaven. His priorities have not changed. They have always required the tangible presence of Holy Spirit to fulfil and they always will. Any teachings, doctrine, or churches who teach any alternate lifestyles or place a higher importance on anything else are likely to become the very vehicle Satan will use to paralyze us from recognizing our true need of God's presence and voice in our lives today. In the next few chapters, we will study on such things I wrestled with from my own upbringing and ministry as a Seventh-day Adventist, in light of the Gospel of demonstration and power.

Eric Gilmour, has been another person God has blessed us to come across. His ministry, *sonship-international.org*, has the latest updates of what Eric is doing now. Two of my favorite books from Eric are: *Union,* and *Enjoying the Gospel.* He not only teaches, but exemplifies a lifestyle, public and private, of one intimately in love and obsessed with the living Christ. He has such a genuine transparent walk with Jesus that will stir your heart and spirit unto a greater intimacy with Jesus.

Jesus is our model. If you want to see what His blood has now made available for us, just look at His life and the things He did and said and realize that same Spirit who possessed Him wants to do the same in you and me today. The presence of the living God inside of us spontaneously produces His life in and through us. His presence is everything. He died to bring life to you and me. Union of God and man once again. Divinely knitted together as one substance, or "one spirit" as the scripture says.

There are many voices out there today. There are many religious teachers, preachers, ministries, churches, and denominations all around us. But the question is, are we following the Lamb? More than likely, you may already attend a church and read from certain authors. But does their life actively demonstrate the presence and intimacy with the living Christ? Do they truly hunger after righteousness, as every follower should? I love surrounding myself with people who are hungrier for Jesus than I am. I love learning from ministries and people who have more fruit than I do.

Such sources can be positively provoking us higher and higher in our walk with Him. I invite you to reevaluate your standard of the Christian life compared to the standard Jesus and His disciples clearly modeled. I invite you to evaluate how much time, trust, honor, and your overall life you give to the Holy Spirit's presence and leading.

How much time do you actually, *practically* spend in His presence? Has it been enough for His presence to truly make a home and rest inside of you? Are you growing from glory to greater glory? Is your walk with Jesus truly adventurous, exciting, fun, and a true joy? Or is it completely predictable, along with your current church activity and those in your religious circle?

If there is one thing on my heart for you to get most from these pages, is a stirring for a greater intimacy with the *living God*. There is nothing and no one like Him. Following Him is hearing His voice, and as we've seen throughout this book, His voice is expressed beyond air passing through vocal cords. He is still living, communicating, healing, delivering, resurrecting, engaging, consuming, reviving, imparting, and supernatural.

When the scripture says, "Seek first the kingdom of God and His righteousness and all these things will be added to you" (Matthew 6:33), you can take it to the bank. The *seeking* is expressed in our diligently seeking to understand and interact with the the Lord Himself, His present presence and voice, and nothing else. When we prioritize time in His presence as priority number one, He will revive, align, and build up your spirit so that you can recognize His tangible Spirit (Holy Spirit) like never before. You'll begin to receive His *living voice* personally expressed to you even more practically real than your own earthly Father. His living presence unlocks everything, including His written Word, which was written by His living presence flowing through mortal men. You will see Him in Scripture like you never have and be found asking yourself, "How could I have missed this?" Dreams, visions, and supernatural encounters will follow, along with a surrendering to Him unlike anything prior, and then that experiencing of His presence begins to overflow in everything you do and onto everyone in you path. Your entire environment, schedule, and all resources get consumed by His presence, and supernatural flourishing, acceleration, and abundant fruit follow as "all these things will be added to you."

You may feel like He's literally breaking you down to nothing, as He purges your character and heart from all the false securities you may not have realized your trust and affections were in, both in the natural and spiritually. You will feel more vulnerable and exposed than ever before, hence, why you will need His tangible presence, Holy Spirit, the Comforter, like never before. What He builds, no man, system, government, religion, can tear down. Our greatest manmade efforts, no matter how humanly valued and appraised, are nothing more than wood, hay, and stubble that will all be burned up as it has no eternal value in the eyes and kingdom of God. But whatever He Himself builds in and through us, lasts for all eternity, as it is good and perfect and from the only sure source, God Himself. He causes us to reflect to the world His goodness, kindness, love, and desire for all His kids, in so many diverse ways.

He loves to work in us in ways that makes men wonder and leaves them in awe of what He has done and how He's done it. He loves to baffle the so called intellectual, humanly esteemed, arrogant religious leaders, and systems of today with His raw, tangible presence, supernatural manifestations, and fruit that spontaneously mark where and with whom He truly is dwelling.

He longs to take us deeper. From glory to greater glory. A life of continuous upgrade after upgrade not only for the next life, but even in this temporary time here on earth, as it models kingdom lifestyle which in turn models the King Himself.

I pray His loving embrace woos you into a place of greater hunger for Him unlike anything before so that He can impart His very self, His living presence into you. The world is groaning for us all as sons and daughters, to burn with our Father's presence in manifest tangible form. They yearn to see a bride (church) who knows her husband's heart intimately and has surrendered her all as a pure bride does for her husband. Out of this intimacy with Jesus, the image of God is birthed through our *practical life* for all the on looking world and universe to see HE IS ALIVE.

PART II - STUDY

True intimacy with Jesus Exposes Our False Religious Idols

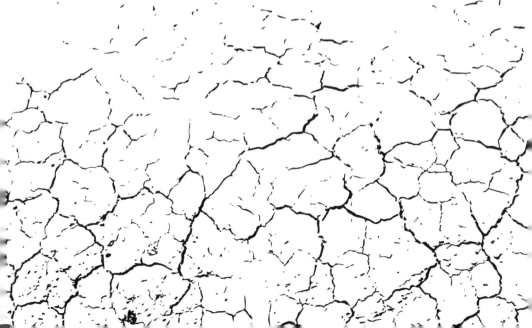

CHAPTER 13

NEW COVENANT REST IN JESUS

Please make sure you have read the chapters leading up to this point. As with anything else, context is very important to a clear and accurate understanding and interpretation. Up to this part of the book, we have been exploring God's invitation and activation for us to experience greater intimacy with Jesus. The following chapters will only be transformational in that context. Outside of intimacy with Him, these chapters will just be mere information and head knowledge, rather than revelation and life-changing transformation.

As we grow in our relationship with Holy Spirit, He takes us to greater and greater levels of surrender and dying to ourselves. He desires full possession of our entire being and lives. If we don't get in His way, He will show us more revelation that leads us into deeper surrender each day.

As God continued to demonstrate Himself to me through personal intimacy followed by more supernatural experiences, He led me back to re-examine specific doctrine that I had grown up with and even faithfully taught and defended as a Seventh-day Adventist evangelist and Bible instructor. I appreciate that, at the time, He didn't start our intimacy by trying to teach me what was entirely right or wrong about my beliefs. It probably would have been a stumbling block for me. But instead, He led me down His priority list, which was tailored to bring me into intimacy with Him.

I know there were many times in my life when I'd be clinging to a particular belief or idea, and He'd win my heart into surrender as He would reveal more of His goodness. He wouldn't even have to directly confront my issue in such cases. They'd be easy to see in the context of His goodness, and no longer qualified to compete for that place in my heart.

At the root of anything that we do not want to surrender to Jesus, is a disbelief that what He wants to exchange is much more valuable than what we hold.

Sometimes, He's willing to give us a glimpse of the greater valued thing He has for us, so that the surrender of what we're clinging to is much easier. Other times, He asks us to surrender first and trust that what He's going to do is of greater value.

Holy Spirit truly is the most qualified guide into all truth, as His priority list for each of us may begin and end with something different, but with the same goal accomplished – intimacy with Jesus, Spirit-to-spirit connection. He knows which things are a stumbling block for you to see and learn about now, versus what you're ready to receive now. He is called the Comforter, because He does stretch us beyond our comfort but gives us the grace and courage to press forward, while trusting Him for revelation and understanding along the way. For me, this is how that priority list of the Holy Spirit unfolded in three steps:

1. After years of doing ministry in various churches, I was convicted of the huge disconnect we had compared to the church in the book of Acts. I couldn't deny Scripture's clear examples and teachings of a Spirit-filled life, compared to the lack in my own life. I thought, "Surely God has to be doing more today than what we are believing He is."

2. I prayerfully began to look for where God was doing the things the early church had described, through what people, and why. I saw the same roots in common with most of the ministries, churches, and individuals I came across. These "on fire" believers lived, being led by the presence of Holy Spirit, and emphasized our need to understand and live from the identity of a redeemed son. They truly applied the Bible in their day-to-day lives, not just reciters of memorized verses and theology. I knew the same verses in my head as they did, but didn't believe them from my heart as they did.

3. I began studying more Bible verses and sermons on our redeemed identity (Dan Mohler's YouTube videos are a great resource and so are the Divine Healing Technician Training YouTube videos from jglm.org ministry). My head knowledge transformed into belief from the heart. As my relationship experience with God changed from "slave/servant" to "son," my expectations and receptivity of supernatural encounters from my heavenly Father also grew.

While spending more time in His presence, I was now learning how to simply *receive* as His son, the way He has always wanted me to. These experiences with His presence made me hungrier and hungrier for more of Him. The hungrier I became for Him, the more willing I was to surrender more of my life, character, and heart to Him. After all, it's the "goodness of God that leads us to repentance," (Romans 2:4). Again, this "order" the Holy Spirit led me on may look different from how He leads and will lead you. But the same goal of greater intimacy will definitely be the byproduct.

In this section, Part II of the book, we are covering teachings, verses, and topics from the Old Testament and see how they have been replaced, enhanced, or expounded on in the New Testament realities we've explored so far in Part I. Such study helped me better examine specific doctrines of my own upbringing (Seventh-day Adventist church) in light of the New Covenant gospel and intimacy with Him.

If you have any kind of religious or Adventist background or influence, I believe it will really resonate with you in your own journey and draw you closer to Him. But even if you don't have any religious background, every human is still born with a sinful nature that seeks to perform for self. This makes *everyone* vulnerable to the various idols religion tries to offer in exchange for greater intimacy with Jesus. Sometimes these religious "idols" or "beliefs" stem back to our childhood and we may not even realize it. The following chapters will display the truths and errors we can fall into with the spirit of religion, regardless of what denomination or church exposure a person has had.

Many religious churches use particular Bible verses to create manmade doctrine to mask their performance-driven activity, but at its root is self-righteousness, pride, and ego. It is important to understand God's written Word, both the Old and New Testaments, in order to avoid religious deceptions, which *seem* to be based on Scripture. Many Christians are following such religious deceptions, truly believing them to be true, but ignorant of their crippling effects on their life and quenching of the Holy Spirit. It was the spirit of religion that worked in the Pharisees and Scribes as they demanded Jesus be put to death and as they later persecuted the early church. Religion attempts to clog our receptivity capacity with false idols and quench the Holy Spirit's ability to guide us into greater intimacy with Jesus.

A few years after the experiences I shared in the first half of this book, God led me to study the book of Hebrews (which I had done many times before) but this time, in light of the Gospel realities I had been experiencing and learning from the Holy Spirit. It's out of revelation stemmed from the book of Hebrews that brought me to the things I share here, in Part II of this book. I pray the Spirit of God would accompany His liberating truths with revelation, power, and breakthrough to you, in Jesus' name.

SABBATH REST

As an Adventist, when I'd hear the term *Sabbath rest,* I'd automatically equate it to mean the "Seventh-day Sabbath." For others, hearing the phrase *Sabbath rest,* may equal Sunday church service or a day. But as you will see soon, God has always invited His people into a Sabbath rest that goes even deeper than what either of these explanations entail. Whether you have an Adventist background or not, you have probably heard of this topic or read verses about the Sabbath, especially in the Old Testament of the Bible. I've come across many people who didn't know how to interpret scriptures like Exodus 31:14, "¹⁴ Ye shall keep the sabbath therefore; for it is holy unto you: every one that defileth it shall surely be put to death." (KJV). *Wow.* That's quite a consequence.

Several Old Testament verses, especially in the story of the Israelites, put a heavy emphasis on the Sabbath as this verse in Exodus does. This can be very alarming when not understood in the biblical and Gospel's context. But I believe, as you discover God's invitation into the Sabbath rest, you'll find yourself enjoying it more than ever.

As an Adventist, the Sabbath is a key doctrine, as the belief is that it represents true law keepers from the false (since it's the fourth commandment of the Ten Commandments), true worship from false (Seventh day of the week, rather than the first), and the end-time seal for God's true last-day church. But how do such beliefs align or undermine the New Covenant realities of the Gospel and the entirety of scripture? How does it affect our belief in Christ's finished work? Or how we view and relate to God and others?

I once was very confident in my understanding of the Sabbath and all of the Scriptures to go to in order to defend the Seventh Day Sabbath. I had preached about the Sabbath, given Bible studies on it, written Bible studies on it, and defended it countless times against other denominations, teachings, and people as a full-time Bible study worker. I knew Sabbath rest was definitely in Scripture and I believed it to have a very important significance, especially in the end times. I did not want to be one of the deceived who would worship the beast on the wrong day. But God had more He wanted to say to me on this topic in relation to the New Covenant realities in Christ.

As I attempt to share with you, in love, what the Holy Spirit has so patiently shared with me, I pray you compare Scripture with Scripture, precept upon precept, in the context of the entire Gospel and New Covenant reality that Jesus' blood has successfully paid for us to enjoy. We will first cover the Sabbath rest and then proceed to other religious doctrines in light of Jesus' New Covenant reality.

A GLIMPSE OF HEBREWS
CHAPTER 3:12-4:16 – THE SABBATH REST

Throughout the whole book of Hebrews, the writer contrasts numerous Old Covenant doctrines with the superior reality in Christ. Hebrews chapters one, two, and the first half of chapter three, contrasts Moses being a servant/slave in that Old Covenant order with Christ being a Son in the New Covenant order. It's in this context, contrasting Old Covenant practices and doctrine versus New Covenant realities, that he touches on the Sabbath rest in chapter 3:12-4:16.

The Sabbath was also a highly regarded doctrine and practice in the Old Covenant which is why it is one of the topics covered in the book of Hebrews. As we examine these verses you will see that the Israelites of the Old Covenant, actually failed to keep or enter into the Sabbath rest despite "obeying" the external aspects of the 4th commandment. We will also see how the Old Covenant Sabbath had a limited experience and understanding compared to the deeper reality and experience that has now come through Jesus. Starting with 3:12 we will see the context preceding the verses about the Sabbath:

The verse starts with the writer encouraging the believers he is writing to.

"Take care, brethren, that there not be in any one of you an evil, unbelieving heart that falls away from the living God. ¹³ But encourage one another day after day, as long as it is still called "Today," so that none of you will be hardened by the deceitfulness of sin."

He then reminds them about their recent acceptance and assurance of the Gospel (the good news) saying:

> *¹⁴ For we have become partakers of Christ, if we hold fast the beginning of our assurance firm until the end,*
>
> What does he mean by, *"if* we hold fast the beginning of our assurance"? The Hebrews were Jews who had lifetimes' worth of religious practices such as animal sacrifices, rituals, the sanctuary requirements and laws, and many other symbolic things that pointed forward to Jesus. Once Jesus came and introduced the Gospel, they were invited to exchange their many symbolic forms for the reality in Jesus. This was difficult, because there were not only used to doing all of that religious activity for so long, but also feared the punishments they had been taught would happen to them if they stopped doing them. The whole book of Hebrews helps the religious Jew (and anyone religious) understand how Jesus is the reality for each of their previously-cherished rituals and beliefs. The goal was to help them "hold fast the beginning of our assurance," which refers to when they first believed in Jesus and His qualifications to be greater than their own works-driven qualifications. Hebrews chapter 3:15-18 continues:
>
> *¹⁵ while it is said,*
> *"TODAY IF YOU HEAR HIS VOICE,*

> Do not harden your hearts, as when they provoked Me."
>
> ¹⁶ For who provoked Him when they had heard? Indeed, did not all those who came out of Egypt led by Moses? ¹⁷ And with whom was He angry for forty years? Was it not with those who sinned, whose bodies fell in the wilderness? ¹⁸ And to whom did He swear that <u>they would not enter His rest</u>, but to those who were disobedient?
>
> The Israelites had been given the Ten Commandments and many other religious duties to help point their faith to Christ. There were serious consequences, including death, if one didn't enter into God's rest on the Sabbath day or during a Sabbath season. In their story you'll find they kept the *form* of the Sabbath, but they missed what the *form* was pointing to. Notice it didn't only say they had disobeyed by "not entering His rest" but how they'd also hardened their hearts to *His voice*.

All through Part I of this book, we've talked about how one could obey an external commandment like the Israelites and Pharisees did and yet reject the present voice of God as they did. Although the Israelites may have thought they had successfully entered God's rest by obeying the external restrictions of the fourth commandment itself, according to God, they actually didn't enter His rest. Chapter 3:19 continues:

¹⁹ So we see that they were not able to enter because of unbelief. Therefore, let us fear if, while a promise remains of entering His rest, any one of you may seem to have come short of it. ² For indeed we have had good news preached to us, just as they also; but the word they heard did not profit them, because it was not united by faith in those who heard. ³ For we who have believed enter that rest.

> Notice the reason *why* God says they didn't enter the reality of that rest? Unbelief. But unbelief in what? 4:2 it says unbelief in the "good news" or Gospel of

Jesus. The fourth commandment of Sabbath rest "did not profit them because it was not united by faith in those who heard." Faith in what? The Gospel. The Sabbath rest mentioned in the fourth commandment was supposed to point the people to a *complete* and *full rest,* which would only be accomplished by the Gospel of Jesus and entered into by faith.

They were invited to put their faith and trust in Him to be their burden carrier and provider of true divine rest. But they didn't believe in the Gospel, which made the commandment powerless since this *rest* wasn't entered into or experienced by merely carrying out the physical aspects of it as they had already been doing.

This passage in Hebrews chapters 3 & 4 emphasizes repetitively that believing in Jesus (His complete work of the New Covenant) equals truly "entering His rest" vs. rejecting Him in unbelief equals "not entering His rest." Later, in 4:8, it even says *the Israelites who were allowed to enter Canaan by Joshua's leadership also did not truly enter that rest.* This is because the Sabbath rest God was con- tinuously inviting His people into, wasn't pointing to a physical place called Canaan, or even just a particular day or time frame in their weekly schedule, but a spiritual divine rest experienced in the New Covenant union with Jesus, as we'll soon see. Just as the sacrifices didn't actually forgive or remove sins and had to be repeated daily and yearly, so the Sabbath was repeated and re-entered into in var- ious ways, *symbolic* of the true rest Christ could only bring.

If you read Leviticus chapters 23 and 25, you'll see God's Sabbath rest invitation extended to the people in various *forms*, specifically after a symbolic *form* of redemptive work or sacrifices. Once a year, a Sabbath rest was to be entered into on The Day of Atonement (signi- fying Jesus' future atonement at the cross) and they were directed to keep it exactly like the seventh-day Sabbath rest instructions. There was also a *year-long Sabbath* they were invited into, which we'll discuss below.

To get the bigger picture, think about this: All year long, the priests would make *daily* animal sacrifices for sins. This would all be carried out in the outer court of the sanctuary and the blood placed into the holy place of the Sanctuary. At the end of each week, they would enter the seventh-day Sabbath and rest from their labors and activity and then re-enter into labor the next day. After a whole year of doing this week after week, a special day called the Day of Atonement would take place. On this Day of Atonement, the high priest would finally enter into the last section of the Sanctuary called the Most Holy Place/Holy of Holies (where God's throne/presence was symbolized by the mercy seat) and transfer all of the activity/sins/labor that had accumulated all year long, into the most Holy Place before God. This was symbolically representing the death of Jesus making a once-and-for-all atonement and payment for all of our sins. They were to enter into a Sabbath rest this day and cease from all their works. Then, (since this was only symbolic still) they would continue the same daily, weekly, and yearly cycle of labor and Sabbaths all over again. In addition to this cycle, there were many other invitations to Sabbath rest, as mentioned in Leviticus 25:

> "And the LORD SPOKE TO MOSES ON MOUNT SINAI, SAYING, ² "Speak to the children of Israel, and say to them: 'When you come into the land which I give you, then the land shall keep a Sabbath to the LORD. ³ Six years you shall sow your field, and six years you shall prune your vineyard, and gather its fruit; ⁴ but in the seventh year there shall be a Sabbath of solemn rest for the land, a Sabbath to the LORD. YOU SHALL NEITHER SOW YOUR FIELD NOR PRUNE YOUR VINEYARD." LEV.25:1-4 NKJV.

Verse 8 also introduces the *year of jubilee Sabbath,* which began on the Day of Atonement and also lasted for an entire year:

> ⁸ 'And you shall count seven Sabbaths of years for yourself, seven times seven years; and the time of the seven Sabbaths of years shall be to you forty-nine years. ⁹ Then you shall cause the trumpet of the Jubilee to sound on the tenth *day* of the seventh month; on the Day of Atonement you shall make the trumpet to sound throughout all your land. ¹⁰ And you shall consecrate the fiftieth year, and proclaim liberty throughout *all* the land to all its inhabitants. Lev. 25:8-10 NKJV.

(Note the number *seven*, which in the Bible is the number of completion and perfection.) If you were supposed to stop working for an entire year, how were you supposed to provide food for your family?

[20] 'And if you say, "What shall we eat in the *seventh year*, since we shall not sow nor gather in our produce?" [21] Then I will command *My blessing* on you in the sixth year, and it will bring forth produce enough for three years. [22] And you shall sow in the eighth year, and eat old produce until the ninth year; until its produce comes in, you shall eat *of* the old *harvest*. Lev.25:20-22 NKJV.

(This is the same principle when God gave them daily mana to eat, which represented Jesus as our Daily bread: on the sixth day, He'd provide *extra* mana so they would not need to go out and gather any on the seventh day). It's only because of God's supernatural, *complete provision* (triple blessing) on the sixth year, that they could truly enter into and enjoy the seventh-year Sabbath. None of their own labors or toil could have ever given them such rest for an entire year.

If this is so clear on these symbolic Old Covenant examples, how much more is the living reality of this through the real atonement for sin – Jesus? None of those sacrifices, sanctuary activities, or blood of animals actually forgave or removed sin, so the Israelites would re-start this seven-year cycle all over again and again, along with the daily and weekly sacrifices and weekly Sabbath rest. The story of Israel has so many symbolic instructions and laws pointing toward New Covenant realities *we now have*.

As we're seeing from Scripture, the Sabbath rest God instructed Israel to keep wasn't merely about the one mentioned in the fourth commandment and, in fact, that paled in comparison to an *entire year of Sabbath* mentioned in the above scriptures. If we'd asked the Israelites, "what is the Sabbath rest and when do we enter it?" they would have probably described each of the different ways God gave them to enter it: weekly, yearly, and seasonally. Each of these various ways of entering the Sabbath rest followed after a symbolic act or acts of redemption. They each pointed forward to Jesus and the complete *"rest"* that would follow after His complete sacrifice.

Before sin came into this world, our existence began and was to continue in Sabbath rest. No toil needed, no striving, no separation from our creator and heavenly Father, complete undivided union with God. The bliss of His presence and peace was the only lifestyle we knew. Let's take a quick look back to that time:

In Genesis chapter 1:5-2:3, for the first six days of creation you see a pattern of each day ending.

"And there was evening and there was morning the first day…" "and there was evening and there was morning the second day…" and so on for six days.

But there is no such closure given on the seventh day. God was very satisfied and pleased with *His* perfect and *complete* (the number seven) labor and work, which he spent the last six days doing for man. But Man, begins his first *full day* of life and existence after all the labor/work was done by God and simply being fully aware of his life source and Father, God. Their complete, right relationship with a Holy God, was the very essence of divine rest. No toiling needed. No striving. Just the enjoyment of being with the one we were created from and for. His presence, unhindered, and enshrouding us with His glory. Man's day-to-day life knew no labor or toil. What was there to work for when all was already supplied and given for their enjoyment?

In Genesis chapters 1 and 2, there is no command given to Adam and Eve to "rest on the seventh day" or "keep the seventh day holy." They would already be doing so by default. It was never God's intention that we would have anything lacking that wasn't already provided and enjoyed in Him and from Him. Their existence began *after His* perfect, completed work had finished. *Adam and Eve's existence knew nothing other than Sabbath rest*, which makes sense why there is no closure mentioned in Genesis 1 for the seventh day, since *it was to be the daily experience of their lives.*

If you fast forward and read all the instructions given on "how to keep the Sabbath" in Leviticus and Deuteronomy, you'd see how a sinless Adam and Eve would have naturally been keeping the Sabbath on day eight and nine and so on. Their sin-free, day-to-day state fulfilled every one of those things and much more. (Besides, any instructions on how to keep the Sabbath were only ever given *after* sin's effects had entered the world, which we'll touch on in the next paragraph.)

Is it possible that God's plan to restore such divine union and Sabbath rest goes deeper than the repetitive symbolic "forms" given to the Israelites? Like so many other forms mentioned in Hebrews, could God have also restored a Sabbath rest through Jesus' death that would go beyond the mere form? A tangible, living reality for our day-to-day life just like Adam and Eve had? I believe the answer is *yes*.

Every Sabbath invitation and instruction given throughout the Old Testament always came *after* some type of *work* had just been completed. When *God first introduced and explained the Sabbath command to the Israelites in Exodus 16:23*, He invited them to "rest" after He supernaturally "worked" to provide food for them. Later, in Exodus 20, He reminded them of that Sabbath command to rest in Exodus 16, and said, *"Remember* the Sabbath day..." This work He invited them to rest from, began for both God and man because of sin. In Gen 3:17b-19, God told Adam that, because of sin,

Cursed is the ground because of you; In *toil* you will eat of it, All the days of your life.18"Both thorns and thistles it shall grow for you; And you will eat the plants of the field;19By the sweat of your face You will eat bread...

The word *toil* mentioned here, in Adam's curse and the word *pain*, referring to the pain Eve was to have in childbirth (Gen 3:16), both are synonymous with the word *labor* in the original text. This *labor* is the result of sin, as it is completely contrary to the rest and peace we were created for, in the presence of God whom we once walked with in the Garden of Eden. The phrase, "six days shall thou *labor* and do all thy *work*," begins to make more sense in context of sin's curse. Physical labor symbolically represented the *labor* sin cursed us with, not merely physically, but spiritually.

In Gen 3:15, we see that Heaven activated the work of salvation from that day forward, and in Scripture, you see *God working* on redeeming that Eden *rest* of union between God and man, from Genesis on. Jesus alluded to this work in John 5, after He'd healed a man on the Sabbath. John 5:16-17 says:

> ¹⁶ For this reason the Jews persecuted Jesus, and sought to kill Him, because He had done these things *on the Sabbath*. ¹⁷ But Jesus answered them, "My Father has been *working until* now, and I have been *working*."

Through every Bible story and historical account, you see examples of what this redemption of Jesus would one day look like in its true, living reality. You see glimpses of divine rest and true worship through people like David, Enoch, and many others. But in Christ, all that was promised, becomes a *living reality* to all who would believe and receive His invitation for divine rest unto the soul. All the physical restraining from in the fourth commandment form, never had the power or ability to bring one's soul into rest. Only the indwelling presence of Jesus experienced through the receiving of the Gospel, can do that.

From the demon-possessed man wandering aimlessly as an outcast seeking rest (Mk 5:1-20), to the inquiring religious leader Nicodemus seeking for something more than what he had experienced with manmade religion (Jn 3), we see the Savior's invitation:

> 28"Come to Me, all who are weary and heavy-laden, and I will give you rest. 29Take My yoke upon you and learn from Me, for I am gentle and humble in heart, and YOU WILL FIND *REST* FOR YOUR *SOULS*. 30For My yoke is easy and My burden is light." -Mat 11:28

Going back to our passage in Hebrews 4:8, it says, "For if Joshua had given them (Israelites) rest, He would not have spoken of _another day_ after that."

What is the "other day" of rest the writer is referring to?

7 He again fixes a certain day, "Today," saying through David after so long a time just as has been said before, "TODAY IF YOU HEAR HIS VOICE, DO NOT HARDEN YOUR HEARTS."

Notice "He (God) *again* fixes a certain day (like He did before in Exodus 20)." This certain day God has fixed is called *today*. His rest isn't symbolically restricted to one physical day of the week like before. As Hebrews points out, even their idea of Sabbath keeping on the seventh day wasn't truly the rest God had invited them into with Christ. But, *today,* we can enter the spiritual reality of the true Sabbath divine rest by *hearing His voice* instead of rejecting it as they did; by believing the Gospel over the old physical order. "For *we who have believed* enter **that** rest..." (Hebrews 4:3)

As sin entered into humanity, it caused separation of sinful man and a Holy God and a discord in our relationship in which our hearts were hardened and ears dull to hearing the voice of God and enjoying the rest of His presence. Like we learned in Part 1 of the book, it was a spiritual disconnect that caused such alienation from a God who is spirit. No matter how many external behavior modifications or instructions of law were given in the Old Covenant, the Israelites modeled it could never reconnect us back to our once-unhindered *hearing of His voice* and walking with Him in the cool of the day, as Adam and Eve once had.

Even years later in the New Testament, the Pharisees and Scribes, who supposedly reverenced and kept the Ten Commandments' law, despised the *voice* of God through Jesus and murdered Him because what He spoke was "blasphemy" against their law and their God.

Please note that it is only possible to hear His voice by close proximity to His very presence and nothing else. It's this union, this spiritual oneness that is finally restored back to man through Jesus. Hearing His voice becomes our *daily* experience as we believe Jesus' methods to be superior than the Old Covenant's methods. We enter true worship of, not just truth, but Spirit and truth (Jn 4). He has given us permanent residence into the very Holy Presence of God. (We'll talk more later about the importance of *hearing His voice* in the section: "Following His Command.")

The old order of things produced a distant worship experience, in which the High priest *alone* would experience *for* the people once a year. It produced an artificial sanctification, of mere physical washings and abstaining from certain physical things, which never cleansed anyone nor had power to bring us into the union they could only symbolize. But Jesus transcends us right into the very arms of the Father. His blood sanctifies us internally as a spiritual new birth and reality *unlike* the first covenant of mere external cleansings and methods. No longer slaves or servants but *sons* given access to the Father with a boldness rather than fear. Intimacy unlike ever before. Rest like back in Eden. Redemption in the fullest sense possible.

The fourth commandment in Ex. 20 shows six days of work preceding the Sabbath ("six days shalt thou *labor* and do all thy work"), because, every new week, there was still "work to be done." This was the experience of the Old Covenant because no sins were truly atoned for, so the daily sacrifices that were done days one to six were again repeated after the Sabbath ended each week. Just as sin/labor brought an end to the divine rest in Eden, so each seventh day Sabbath would come to an end so that labor could restart once again each week. It fits right in with the sin conscious realities of the Old Covenant. A person under that covenant is obviously more conscious of their six days of labor compared to their one day of rest.

To continue to remain in that same cycle today, is to put ourselves back under the Old Covenant era as to say, "I must still labor again." It's to deny the completion of Jesus full and complete "once and for all" atonement, and in unbelief reject the rest that He invites us into "today," as our permanent experience from now throughout eternity.

As mentioned earlier, Lev 23:26-27 also shows the people were instructed to enter a Sabbath rest on the Day of Atonement. Being that this Day of Atonement didn't actually "atone" for anyone's sins, (it was symbolic), it had to be repeated year after year, and that Sabbath rest re-entered into each time after. But Jesus' death, which the Day of Atonement symbolically pointed to, has atoned us once and for all, and therefore the *true Sabbath rest can be the permanent experience for every believer who believes today.*

It's important to note that the Sabbath rest of the New Covenant is what the seventh day Sabbath *and* other Sabbath forms were always pointing us to. This transition from the physical form to spiritual reality of the Sabbath was a struggle for many Jews considering they had a lifetime's worth of keeping the form of the Sabbath. Hence why verses like this were given as guidance:

> "[16] Therefore no one is to act as your judge in regard to food or drink or in respect to a festival or a new moon or a Sabbath day— [17] things which are a *mere* shadow of what is to come; but the substance belongs to Christ." -Colossians 2:16, 17 NASB.

> God doesn't destroy Sabbath rest, but contrary, He can now bring us into its very reality in Christ. Prior to the cross, that reality could only be symbolically represented and looked forward to just like everything else in the Old Covenant. Just as the context of the book of Hebrews' is contrasting the powerless forms of the Old Testament/Covenant vs. their spiritual fulfillment and reality in Christ, so it includes the form of the seventh day Sabbath (which symbolically

contained rest into a physical day) being surpassed with the very substance of Sabbath rest – the presence of Jesus Himself.

My personal experience of New Covenant Sabbath rest has continued to unfold into greater and greater living realities. I first saw how natural this rest came, the more I grew in becoming aware of His tangible presence and present voice. My appetite for secular things diminished more and more and my hunger for Him continued to surpass everything else. I went from a fast food-like devotion time to three to five hours each morning with Him, because I felt like His presence was irresistible.

As Holy Spirit began to lead me into a deeper, more genuine, worship lifestyle from the secret place, I found this pull from deep within, to give God more surrender, more praise, more adoration than ever before. I didn't need a hype man or worship leader, a specific beat or tune, because His tangible presence by itself can do all the provoking to us needed. His Spirit was awakening my spirit to the realization that "today," HE IS HERE. I then found this personal worship overflowing throughout my day, in the car, and in corporate worship services. The more I am consumed with His presence and who He is, the less consumed I am with all the self-conscious fears of "What will the person sitting next to me think if I raise both of my hands?" I slowly began to realize just how paralyzing religion had been to worshiping from my spirit. I had never known how to, nor was I provoked in any way, to desire something more genuine, since it seemed like everyone else in our circle was okay with the same degree that I was.

All throughout Scripture, we see accounts of human beings who have encounters with the living God that leaves them in awe and wonder of who He is, and then causes them to spontaneously respond in worship. David expressed his joy from the Lord by dancing unashamed, with just an undergarment, before his whole city. His own self-awareness and self-consciousness were eclipsed by a superior awareness of the living God. And so, I began to experience a freedom unlike anything before. A freedom from all the critical, judgmental, worrisome, fearful garbage that had distracted my affections and gaze from the one whom they were designed to adore. Whenever we are "holding ourselves together" for the sake of our own human pride and dignity, what we are really saying is, "He's not worth me giving this up." Self remains very much alive as we continue to cater to the appeals of our own human pride, dignity, and fear of man. Whenever we label or cast a judgment on someone else for the way they are worshipping God, we are saying, "Okay, God can't be *that good* to cause you to do that."

From the beginning, the devil envied the worship and adoration that God received and, since then has done anything and everything possible to keep us from adoring our heavenly Father the way He truly deserves. Worship goes beyond any particular form, or even any particular day of worship – it's an actual lifestyle. Apart from a preceding lifestyle of worship, there's no hunger, no passion, no self-abandonment before the Lord.

Instead, a form of polished people reciting the words off a screen or hymnal, while our thoughts, affections, and worries are about any and everything else consuming us. But please understand, it's not the physical raising of hands, clapping, etc. that makes the difference I'm referring to here. In fact, the last thing God wants us to do is pretend to be so into Him in public, while in private we're actually not. That's just hypocrisy and it may fool the believers around us but it is definitely not fooling Him. But it's a genuine surrender of our lives to God in private, in the secret place, that overflows into our worship in public. The by-product is a more expressive, or in-tune worship, that overflows from the heart and our day-to-day life experience with God, rather than the head. The religious form is completely numbing to our spiritual senses which are the very receptors for His Spirit and His practical presence. No wonder there's such a lack of engagement with His presence in religious services. It's doing the church thing, and it's widely practiced and embraced week after week, worldwide, despite the clear lack of tangible supernatural presence and fruit that God is truly welcomed there to do as He pleases the ways He pleases.

But corporate church worship is incredibly powerful when we have each spent intimate hours alone in private with Jesus throughout the week and then bring each of our individual overflow of God into one place. I've seen countless people even be instantly healed of sickness in such an environment, without anybody even having to pray or lay hands on them. Such is a testament to God's presence being there. I've even seen the complete difference in how my son reacted at age two, and now at three, when the presence of God is tangibly in a worship service vs. a religious service. When God's presence is there, He is miraculously engaged with worship for an entire hour with us. Even when we've tried to get him to go to the kid's class, he wants to stay in the worship until it's completely finished. But in the fifteen-minute religious worship service, he's completely distracted and wanting to leave to go play.

Although I saw the initial fruits of New Covenant Sabbath rest from a spiritual perspective, this began to overflow into other practical areas of life. I began to see His invitation to *rest* more fully in Him with fitness/health, money, work, and other areas of my life. I began to see, the deeper into His rest I went, the easier it was to let go of my control and surrender to His Lordship and leadership. Time I'd once wasted on certain worries, anxieties, and activities was exchanged for time with Jesus. It didn't feel like a religious discipline as the *form* had. It felt like an utmost delight. Anytime I'd get free time or have the house to myself on a rare occasion, I'd want to spend it with Him. His presence truly is that good.

I can't share all the examples this continues to flow into but for example with finances, He challenges us beyond the tithing of 10% each week. We began to experience a deeper rest, which allows us to learn to listen for how much to give and to whom to give any and every time an opportunity to give came up. This seemed to come much easier for my wife, but for me this has been a struggle for my flesh, as I feared that being so vulnerable to God in this area of finances would stretch me beyond my level of belief. He truly does, but if there is anybody qualified to control this area, it's Him. Hence the need for deeper rest and trust in Him as our provider, rather than trust in my job or paycheck. Sometimes He'd convict us to give an amount that was supposed to pay our mortgage and other times something much smaller, but we've been learning to rest by surrendering our control (it's easier for our flesh to follow a formula like 10% tithe) in exchange for His present voice to guide us. I believe this is vital to growing past the control money has on so many of us, and step into the double portion, supernatural abundance and prosperity God always provided, preceding deeper Sabbath rest.

Despite these revelations about the New Covenant Sabbath rest lifestyle vs. Old Covenant form, I still had so many questions for God regarding other scriptures and teachings I'd taught for years in ministry. A part of me (my spirit) felt like it was receiving greater life and light, but my soul/mind was struggling to accept it. After all, I'd read and heard countless warnings from our church leadership about deviating from our understanding of the seventh day Sabbath. But thankfully, the Holy Spirit didn't leave me in such a conflicted state, but instead continued to show me from Scripture further revelation, which drew me into deeper intimacy with Him. Regardless of your belief and stance, I pray He is leading you into the same result: greater intimacy with Him.

CHAPTER 14

COVENANT SIGNS IN SCRIPTURE

After coming to the revelation I'd shared in Chapter 13, I thought to myself, "But doesn't the seventh day Sabbath have a unique emphasis in scripture *unlike* the other "forms?" I studied to see what the whole context of Scripture had to say about this. The more I studied this topic, the more questions I had regarding certain texts I had always used to defend the seventh day Sabbath keeping. The Old Testament has verses where God told the people if they broke the Sabbath they were to be put to death or "cut off." There are also Scriptures that talk about the Sabbath being a sign of the law and Mosaic Covenant for "generations to come." Is there any such equal emphasis in Scripture regarding anything else like this, or is it unique to the seventh day Sabbath the way I and my church had always taught?

I was blown away when I began to see how incredibly parallel certain Scriptures and commands are for both circumcision and the Sabbath.

I believed, along with other Adventists, that circumcision was not relevant in the New Covenant, but rather Christ has brought us into what that form/symbol represented, which is a circumcision of the heart. This is clearly affirmed in scriptures like this:

> ²⁸ For he is not a Jew who is one outwardly, nor is circumcision that which is outward in the flesh. ²⁹ But he is a Jew who is one *inwardly*; and circumcision is that which is of the *heart*, by the Spirit, not by the letter; and his praise is not from men, but from God. Romans 2:28-29 NASB.

We applaud Paul when, in Galatians and other passages, he would elaborate the need to forsake the powerless form in exchange for its spiritual reality in Christ and how not forsaking it puts you right back under the condemnation of the law and Old Covenant order. But in light of my study, I began to wonder if we'd done that exact mistake with the seventh day Sabbath. Please note the contrasts below of how circumcision is referred to and how the seventh day Sabbath is referred to in these passages. *You'll see that just as circumcision was the sign one would have to keep or perform, in order to be included in Abraham's covenant/promises, the seventh day Sabbath was also a sign that one would keep to be identified in the Covenant of Moses.*

CIRCUMCISION

Genesis 17:9-13 NASB:

> [9] God said further to Abraham, "Now as for you, you shall keep My covenant, you and your descendants after you throughout their generations. [10] This is My covenant, which you shall keep, between *Me and you and your [u]descendants after you*: every male among you shall be circumcised. [11] And you shall be *circumcised* in the flesh of your foreskin, and it shall be *the sign of the covenant between Me and you.* [12] And every male among you who is eight days old shall be circumcised *throughout your generations*, a *servant* who is born in the house or who is bought with money from any foreigner, who is not of your [k] descendants. [13] A *servant* who is born in your house or who is bought with your money shall surely be circumcised; thus shall *My covenant be in your flesh for an everlasting covenant.*

SEVENTH DAY SABBATH

Exodus 31:12-18

> [12] The LORD SPOKE TO MOSES, SAYING, [13] "But as for you, speak to the sons of Israel, saying, 'You shall surely observe My Sabbaths; for *this* is *a sign between Me and you throughout your generations*, that you may know that I am the LORD WHO SANCTIFIES YOU. [14] Therefore you are to observe the Sabbath, for it is holy to you. Everyone who profanes it shall surely be put to death; for whoever does any work on it, that person shall be cut off from among his people. [15] For six days work may be done, but on the seventh day there is a Sabbath of complete rest, holy to the LORD; WHOEVER DOES ANY WORK ON THE SABBATH DAY SHALL SURELY BE PUT TO DEATH. [16] So the sons of Israel shall observe the Sabbath, to [a]celebrate the Sabbath throughout their generations as a *perpetual covenant*.' [17] It is a *sign* between Me and the sons of Israel forever; for in six days the LORD MADE HEAVEN AND EARTH, BUT ON THE SEVENTH DAY HE CEASED *FROM LABOR*, and was refreshed." [18] When He had finished speaking with him upon Mount Sinai, He gave Moses the two tablets of the testimony, tablets of stone, written by the finger of God."

I once used to emphasize the term "perpetual covenant" or "eternal sign" in the above text when speaking of the seventh day Sabbath. However, one cannot ignore the same *exact* words and terminology is used in regard to the "sign" of circumcision and yet, I'd find myself denying the same interpretation for the circumcision passage. However, basic Bible interpretation requires that what we apply for one we do for both if we seek accurate and unbiased Bible interpretation. Notice the contrasts of these two signs side by side:

Circumcision: "You shall keep my covenant" –Gen17:9

Sabbath: "You shall surely observe my Sabbath"-Ex 31:13

Circumcision: "Me and you and your descendants"- Gen 17:9

Sabbath: "Me and the sons of Israel" –Ex 31:17

Circumcision: "And you shall be circumcised" –Gen 17:11

Sabbath: "You are to observe the Sabbath"-Ex 31:14

Circumcision: "Throughout your generations"-Gen 17:12

Sabbath: "Throughout your generations" Ex 31:13

Circumcision: "The sign...between Me and you" Gen 17:11

Sabbath: "A sign between Me and you" Ex 31:13

Circumcision: "An everlasting covenant" Gen 17:13

Sabbath: "A perpetual covenant" Ex 17:14

Circumcision: "Uncircumcised...cut off" Gen 17:14

Sabbath: "Whoever does any work...cut off" Ex 31:14

Circumcision: "Servant to be circumcised" Gen 17:12

Sabbath: "Servant to keep the Sabbath" Ex 20:10

Circumcision: Sign of circumcision given at the time of giving the covenant Gen 17:1-9

Sabbath: "Sign of Sabbath given at the time of giving of the covenant Ex 31:18

Circumcision mentioned 6 times

Sabbath mentioned 6 times

Galatians, Hebrews, and many other places in New Testament Scripture show us the importance of truly believing the Gospel over the Old Covenant order. As I was seeing this in Scripture, I found myself saying, "Well, maybe I can keep the seventh day Sabbath and New Covenant Sabbath." However, one completely nullifies and contradicts the other. One is physical, the other spiritual. One is form, the other reality and fulfillment. One has only symbols, the other tangible, transformational power. God was gracious with me in my journey, as I wrestled with many years of emphasizing the seventh day Sabbath scriptures and Adventist beliefs. But the more I experienced of His presence and voice, the more rest I lived my *entire daily life* from, rather than one day out of the week. This made the contrast of Old Covenant Sabbath vs. New Covenant Sabbath so much easier for me to see first-hand, by experience. One is external instruction to be "done" as a work, the other a work Jesus accomplished to now be *received*. One condemns, the other redeems. One enslaves, the other liberates and frees. One magnifies the distance sin has caused us from God (six days of labor with only one day of rest), the other destroys the distance and unites us closer than ever before.

As a kid, I would have described the Sabbath to you as all the things I couldn't or wasn't supposed to do on that day, in order to keep it holy. As I a teen, despite keeping the seventh day form by not working on the seventh day, I continued to be void of the *rest* it had always pointed forward to in Jesus. Subconsciously, I truly prioritized the keeping of the *form* over the practical time I spent with Jesus. Although I would have told you differently with my words, my life expressed, "Regardless of how spiritual I am or not right now, I'll be safe because I know to side with the group who's keeping the seventh day." So, although I would party, smoke weed, and drink, "at least I'm not working on the seventh day." So many of my peers from Adventist Academy and college would do the same. Hanging tightly to a form, while void of the presence of the one it had always pointed to – Jesus.

Israel rejected the Sabbath rest invitation by unbelief. And so is the challenge today... do we believe the symbols will give me true rest or Jesus? Do our lives show that we truly believe His blood enough? Is His presence not superior to the Old Covenant means? Do we try to put new wine into old wine skins? Or will we simply believe and receive the Gospel? Could this deeper rest truly be a living reality in which our very life testifies that we are resting in the abiding presence of the prince of peace Himself?

Eventually later on, when Christ brought me out of my rebellion and into the beginning of experiencing the gospel, I highly regarded the seventh day Sabbath. Nothing you could say or show me would persuade me differently, because I believed more than anything the devil wanted me to be deceived into disregarding the seventh day Sabbath as so many *other* Christians had. To me, disregarding the seventh day Sabbath would equal breaking the law and the separating factor of God's true church in the end of times. I had believed that the New Covenant was accomplished to point me back to the law so that I could be a better law keeper. But, in reality, my thought process believed it was making us better slaves, or servants, rather than the supernatural adoption of sons. How contrary this is to verses like Gal 3:19, 24 that clearly says:

Why the Law then? It was added because of transgressions, having been ordained through angels by the agency of a mediator,

until the seed would come to whom the promise had been made...
Therefore the Law has become our tutor *to lead us to Christ,* so that
we may be justified by faith.

(See also, Galatians 4:21-31 which contrasts the Old Covenant
law vs. New Covenant reality, "servant/slave" vs "son," by comparing
the "fleshly" work of Hagar's pregnancy versus the "spiritual work"
of Sarah's birth of Isaac, the child of promise.)

When we view the topic of *covenants* in context of the whole Bible,
we see the following divine *pattern:* God made a covenant with Noah
never to flood the earth again and gave the **rainbow** to him as a *sign* of
that covenant (Gen 9:8-17). God made a covenant with Abraham and gave
circumcision to him as a *sign* of that covenant (Gen 17:9-13). God made a
covenant with Moses and the Israelites and gave the **seventh day Sabbath**
to them as a *sign* of that covenant (Ex 31:12-18). Just like the other covenants between God and man prior, the seventh day Sabbath was the *sign*
given to be remembered and observed in order to be identified with the
Mosaic covenant and law.

Scripturally there is no greater emphasis of the *seventh day
Sabbath sign* given to Israel over any of the previous signs given to
Abraham or Noah. *Scripturally,* they all pointed to a superior fulfill-
ment and actualization of it in Christ. Nowhere in *any* of the New
Testament writings of Paul or other disciples or apostles is this sev-
enth day sign emphasized or instructed to be carried over into the
New Covenant or end time events to come. In fact, like we saw in
Hebrews 3 and 4, they emphasize its total completion in Christ *just
as they do* for circumcision and other Old Covenant *forms.*

In light of these things, I couldn't help but wonder, "Well then
when and how did this exclusive magnification of the seventh Day
Sabbath form begin in our church?" I studied further into the context
of the Adventist pioneers and found from when and how they first
began to emphasize and teach the seventh day Sabbath. It began
from this Ellen G. White vision regarding the Ten Commandments:

"But the fourth (the Sabbath commandment,) shone above
them all; for the Sabbath was set apart to be kept in honor of God's
holy name. The holy Sabbath looked glorious – a halo of glory was
all around it. I saw that the Sabbath was not nailed to the cross."
–1EGWLM 113.1

If you research it for yourself, you'll find that, up until this point
in time (mid 1800's) the Adventist pioneers had *not been keeping the*

seventh day Sabbath. They went to church on Sundays as the other Christians did. They didn't discover the seventh day Sabbath form by studying the Bible more thoroughly than the other Christians around them, which is what I had always believed. Instead it was due to a vision one person had and other visions she would later emphasize, that the pioneers submitted themselves back into the Old Covenant form, seventh day Sabbath. Her *exclusive* revelation was embraced as being from the Lord despite its contradiction of the New Covenant realities and New Testament scriptures which clearly condemn returning back to Old Covenant forms. Paul says, in Galatians 1:8 , "But even if we, or an *angel from heaven*, should preach to you a gospel contrary to what we have preached to you, he is to be accursed."

*As an Adventist, I started to realize, that in order to maintain Adventist theology of the seventh day Sabbath and end times, as we have believed, we have to place our faith and trust in the visions and writings of Ellen White and the other Adventist pioneers, in order to have the emphasis **they say** to have on these points. They alone placed this emphasis of the seventh day Sabbath, although there is no such emphasis in the New Covenant or New Testament, and no other church/group during their era who was inspired by God to do the same.*

In my journey with the Holy Spirit, I've become an even bigger believer of signs, wonders, miracles and visions. I've found He actually wants more of us to experience these things on a regular basis just like the early church of Acts. But we always have to test everything supernatural by scripture. If it's truly of the Lord His word will confirm it. But if it isn't, the vision or dream will contradict what the scripture is saying.

I wondered, "Why would the Adventist pioneers be so vulnerable to follow a drastic doctrinal change like this despite its contradiction to Scripture?" If you study into the timeline and process of EGW and the pioneers regarding these isolated conclusions, you'll find this change took place shortly after they had taught Jesus was coming in 1844 and were proven to be in error. This is also a time when many other denominations were beginning to form and people were desperately searching for truth.

You can imagine there must have been many people following their leadership when they were teaching them to prepare for Jesus' coming in 1844. Then you can imagine after that, the huge disappointment that immediately followed along with a huge loss of their spiritual credibility among other Christians. The Adventist pioneers had believed they had something unique that *set them apart from all the other Christians*, only to be proven wrong. Shortly after that experience they now have another *unique revelation* (seventh day Sabbath) that invites their remaining followers to be *set apart* from everyone else – *once again*. In fact, when you read the numerous visions she has regarding the Sabbath, Ten Commandments, and so forth, she taught the emphasis of them from her exclusive revelation, and as such important truths that accepting them brought you into the remnant and true church of God but rejecting them meant you would be lost. Imagine the fear that caused with so many people genuinely seeking for the truth. Imagine the criticisms from other Bible-believing Christians that E.G.W and the Adventist pioneers would have to defend against using her *exclusive* insight to justify their isolation. As the pillar doctrines of Adventism would continue to unfold, you will find her exclusive and isolated visions and authority were leading the way. Adventists would find themselves having to believe not only in Jesus but in EGW's *exclusive* visions and authority. Apart from it, they had no true biblical justification for their *emphasis* of particular scripture used to support their *unique* doctrines.

We will discuss more about E.G.W and Adventist history later in our study, but it's important to realize that such *emphasis* of the seventh day Sabbath contradicts the complete gospel that the writer of Hebrews, Galatians, and many other New Testament books clearly present.

I also thought to myself, "Didn't Jesus keep the seventh day Sabbath?" But, if you dig further into the context He was raised into, you find He was also circumcised on the eighth day, and scripture shows Him and His parents following all the other feasts and temple ordinances of the Old Covenant. That is because the New Covenant wasn't inaugurated or "put into effect" until His blood was shed and He rose from the dead.

Lk 22:19-20 records while Jesus is with His disciples at the last supper, He instructs them of how we are to remember the New Covenant:

[19] "And when He had taken *some* bread *and* given thanks, He broke it and gave it to them, saying, "This is My body which is given for you; *do this* in remembrance of Me." [20] And in the same way *He took* the cup after they had eaten, saying, "This cup which is poured out for you is the *New Covenant* in My blood.

> This very act that we now call *communion* is what we New Covenant believers do to remember all that Christ has ended and begun by the shedding of His blood. When we partake of communion we are saying, "I believe, receive, and identify myself with the New Covenant through Jesus' blood."

I invite you to pray this prayer out loud to Jesus:

Jesus, I thank you for your blood. I long to understand the depths of what Your death truly means for my personal life today. I ask Holy Spirit to guide me into the realities of the New Covenant and lead my heart to surrender more fully to You. Transform my life into one that holds nothing back from You. Help me to let go of any and every religious form that I've put my trust in, in exchange of Your blood. In Jesus' name,

Amen.

I felt like I was getting more clarity from Scripture and the Holy Spirit regarding this topic. But I still feared fully embracing these truths would equal missing out on the end times protection/seal,

which I'd always believed was the seventh day Sabbath form.

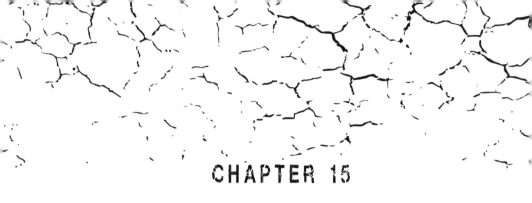

CHAPTER 15

THE BELIEVER'S DIVINE SEAL

What about the seal or sign aspect of the Sabbath regarding the last days? As an Adventist, my belief was that the seventh day Sabbath would be the very seal or sign that would stamp God's true people and church apart from the false, specifically in the last days. In fact, this is one of Adventism's pinnacle beliefs that separates it from all other denominations, hence why it is so highly regarded and protected in the church. I used to believe one of the main focuses of the devil's overall plan was to try and deceive us into rejecting the Sabbath. After all, he was successful in executing that plan in all the existing Sunday churches already, so as church leaders we'd stress the importance of sticking together so that we too don't get led astray. But over time I've seen how it's that very fear tactic of the devil that has crippled so many genuine Adventist and other religious organizations from enjoying the pure gospel of Jesus Christ. When any religious form or symbol is prioritized and proudly worn as a distinguishing seal or sign, it's typically in exchange of the very person and presence of the Holy Spirit. When there's such a lack of the Holy Spirit's presence, we come up with theories to try and reason *why*. One theory I used to believe is:

"Signs and wonders are *not needed* anymore because we have the written Word now."

The result? Religious services, Old Covenant beliefs, and form without power. His *written word* is of utmost importance but it never came as a replacement of His *living word*. In fact, His written word constantly promotes a living relationship with His tangible presence and voice throughout scripture; it doesn't replace it. Hence why Jesus' ministry was filled with an abundance of signs and wonders, as they reveal the heart and living voice of the Father to His children in the present day.

The Holy Spirit continued to challenge my beliefs about the Sabbath as a last day seal of God's *true* church. He spoke to my heart one day and said, "When was the last time you went to your church and saw *any* of the nine gifts of the Holy Spirit? (These are: *word of wisdom, the word of knowledge, increased faith, the gifts of healing, the gift of miracles, prophecy, the discernment of spirits, diverse kinds of tongues, interpretation of tongues.* -1Cor. 12) It's one thing if, over the course of more than 150 years, this list is at least developing in the church more and more, but to be in the same stagnant state and not think of it as a problem, is a huge red flag.

The truth is I was so used to doing church without *any* manifestations of Holy Spirit's presence. Truthfully, if anyone would have begun to minister or exhibit any of the above gifts, I'd likely have labeled them as deceived or demonic rather than being of God. But that same response is the one the religious Jews gave Jesus and His disciples all throughout the New Testament whenever they would minister with the endorsing presence and power of Holy Spirit. I remember when I would come across such a person from outside of the church, no matter how Christ-like, loving, and amazing they would seem I'd subconsciously be saying to myself, "Yeah, but they don't have the truth, so be careful because they may try to deceive you."

I've now personally witnessed and can testify of *many* other churches and ministries outside of Adventism where Holy Spirit's presence is truly allowed to operate. The difference of church in that setting is incredible. It truly parallels the numerous scriptural accounts of what church is supposed to look like when God's tangible presence is honored and desired to be the *central focus* rather than man-made traditions, programs, and forms.

We often use such heightened skepticisms and human rationalizations to avoid facing the obvious lack of the Holy Spirit's presence in the church and in ourselves. However, scripture warns us of that exact religious mindset and system being the last day deception:

...in the last days difficult times will come... holding to a *form of godliness, although they have denied its power;* Avoid such men as these 2Ti 3:1,5.

I began to study for any biblical proof of Moses' Old Covenant seal (seventh Day Sabbath) continuing on into the New Covenant as a seal for the end time believer. Could it be one of the forms of godliness mentioned in that last text? I found that if the seventh day Sabbath was carried over into the New Covenant and magnified to be the "end time seal of God's true church," this would completely contradict the Gospel and the New Testament's clear distinguished differences between the Old and New Covenants. If we believe salvation is by grace through faith alone how do we reconcile that with the idea that in the last days God's people will <u>then</u> be distinguished by those keeping the seventh day Sabbath but those who reject it identified with the mark of the beast? It's as if we're saying, "Well, for now, it's salvation by grace through faith alone, but in the last days that will change and the Sabbath will then be the salvation issue, as the keeping of it will be the sign or seal of God's true church."

But wouldn't there be at least *one* New Testament writer who would emphasize that if it was true? Wouldn't someone like the apostle Paul who was a high-ranking Pharisee of the Ten Commandment Law and who had all the books of Moses memorized by the age of fourteen, touch on such an important point in at least one of his thoroughly written New Testament books? Instead we see a very opposite approach in Paul's writings. An approach that shifted when Jesus Himself appeared on his journey to Damascus and laid him flat on his back. I could only imagine the huge shock of Paul's previous followers and colleagues to hear and see his new disregard for all their laws and traditions in exchange for his discovered Savior and Lord Jesus Christ. Listen to his heart in these verses:

> [2] Beware of the *dogs*, beware of the evil workers, beware of the false circumcision; [3] for we are the *true* circumcision, who *worship in the Spirit of God* and glory in Christ Jesus and *put no confidence in the flesh*,[4] although I myself might have confidence even in the flesh. If anyone else has a mind to put confidence in the flesh, I far more: [5] circumcised the eighth day, of the nation of Israel, of the tribe of Benjamin, a Hebrew of Hebrews; *as to the Law, a Pharisee;* [6] as to zeal, a persecutor of the church; *as to the righteousness which is in the Law*, found blameless.[7] But whatever things were gain to me, those things I have counted as loss for the sake of Christ. [8] More than that, I count all things to be loss in view of the *surpassing*

value of knowing Christ Jesus my Lord, for whom I have suffered the loss of all things, and count them but *rubbish* so that I may gain Christ, [9] and may be found in Him, not having a righteousness of my own derived from *the* Law, but that which is through faith in Christ, *the righteousness which comes from God on the basis of faith*, [10] *that I may know Him* and the power of His resurrection and the fellowship of His sufferings, being conformed to His death;[11] in order that I may attain to the resurrection from the dead. Philippians 3:2-11 NASB.

Notice that he equates, "putting confidence in the flesh" with all of the law-keeping practices that were "once gain to him." Notice his emphasis on the need to "count those things as loss/rubbish in view of the surpassing value of knowing Christ Jesus." That's what this is all about. What are we striving to value more? What are we working so hard to defend? What Moses did or Jesus? What the law could or couldn't do or the Holy Spirit? There is an experiential knowing of Christ that He desires to bring us into. There's an intimacy with Jesus that shifts our perspective to be in alignment with His. It's in experiencing such a relationship with Him that it becomes easy to regard as rubbish the religious beliefs and practices our flesh so dearly prizes.

It's not a disregard for morals but a deeper application from the inside out.

We surrender up the value and faith we once put into the Law by putting our faith in Christ. We receive His gift of the indwelling Holy Spirit so that Holiness becomes the natural byproduct of His presence, rather than my religious efforts.

If God was truly reinstating such an Old Covenant sign of the seventh day Sabbath in the last days why would we see such an abundance of scripture saying the complete opposite as we've seen in our study? Why would He take us back to a *physical symbolism* when the *spiritual reality* of the Sabbath rest has now come in Christ?

Although Adventist theology teaches the seventh Day Sabbath is the end time seal let's see what scripture actually teaches us about how the we are sealed as New Covenant believers and beneficiaries:

> Now He who establishes us with you in Christ and anointed us is God,[22] who also *sealed* us and gave *us* the *Spirit* in our hearts *as a pledge*. -2Cor. 1:21-22

> [13] In Him, you also, after listening to the message of truth, the gospel of your salvation—having also believed, you *were sealed* in Him with the Holy Spirit of promise, [14] who is given as a pledge of our inheritance, with a view to the redemption of *God's own* possession, to the praise of His glory. Eph. 1:13-14

> [30] Do not grieve the Holy Spirit of God, *by whom you were sealed* for *the day of redemption.* Eph. 4:30

> [16] The *Spirit Himself* testifies with our spirit that we are children of God, [17] and if children, heirs also, heirs of God and fellow heirs with Christ, if indeed we suffer with *Him* so that we may also be glorified with *Him*. Ro 8:16-17 NASB.

The seal given to us in the New Covenant is far superior to any previous seals or signs the Old Covenant used, because it's the very presence of God Himself, the Holy Spirit.

The Holy Spirit is the only seal or sign Scripture teaches regarding our inheritance from the New Covenant. Nowhere in the New Testament does it say it's the Sabbath or any other keeping of the physical law of circumcision or sanctuary services. In fact, scripture condemns us from believing so. There is *only* one unpardonable sin mentioned in the New Covenant – rejecting or blaspheming Holy Spirit:

"[29] but whoever blasphemes against the Holy Spirit never has forgiveness, but is guilty of an eternal sin"—" Mk. 3:29.

The issue now goes much deeper than, "What have you done with the fourth commandment?" Instead it's, "What have you done with My presence, the Holy Spirit?" That's why we have instruction in the New Testament: do not grieve the Holy Spirit. Despite the Jews history of laws they were given, the true followers and people of God in the New Testament were those who received and experienced a living relationship with His Son Jesus. Jesus was the actual embodiment of God's presence, and when He left, He sent His Spirit who is currently God's tangible presence on the earth today.

The more revelation I continued to grow in, the more convicted I was that what I had defended and protected for so long was the very system of beliefs quenching the active work of the Holy Spirit in my life and of so many others. He wanted more possession of my heart, character, and life, not just my religious theology. He wants to manifest Himself, both inside and out of us, because Jesus paid the ultimate price to take permanent residence in us. He truly is *enough*, and when He's allowed to truly be Lord over the entirety of our lives, the fruit is genuine, pure, and filled with holiness.

I've personally seen, that the more I have truly believed and embraced the realities of the New Covenant over my previous trust and securities of the Old Covenant, the more intimacy with God I have experienced. I've seen first-hand that His supernatural manifestations of power, signs, wonders, dreams, and visions have not ceased, but are found only through intimacy with His presence. As we dive further into New Covenant realities, Holy Spirit reveals how spiritually bankrupt we are, if we're trying to maintain the hollow shell of Old Covenant methods and beliefs. For me, this truly has been a process as the Holy Spirit has taken me through each Old Covenant principle, one by one, revealing what I was putting my faith in, instead of Him. It's no wonder He is so quenched and hindered to be Himself in most any religious organizations that make the same mistake.

Jesus said, "You will know them by their fruits…"

The entire book of Hebrews and the New Testament so clearly contrasts the Old Covenant and *all* the laws contained in it, pointed *forward* to Christ, not the other way around. When we fall into the trap of legalism and religiosity, as many Jews in New Testament times, we subject ourselves under a powerless covenant and experience. Unfortunately, this mistake is often the very experience of so many religious churches and organizations today. However, in the New Covenant, Jesus invites into a very powerful, tangible, relationship that supersedes any previous era up till now.

I invite you to pray this prayer out loud:

Father, I pray you help me to believe that Your Holy Spirit is truly qualified enough to be the one that testifies that I am Your sealed son/daughter. Help me to release my grip on any false religious securities I've been relying on as endorsements from You. Rearrange what I value and prioritize, so that my heart and beliefs will be surrendered to Your Spirit, rather than quenching it.

In Jesus' name,

Amen.

CHAPTER 16

FOLLOW HIS COMMAND

One of the things I used to teach and preach on, is the importance of the Ten Commandment Law for today. The common belief we had, as Adventists, was that the majority of Christians were disobeying the Ten Commandments, since they weren't following the fourth one, about the Sabbath Day, like we were.

This was a key difference in what we believed as a denomination, apart from the majority of Christianity today. I had numerous scriptures I'd point to as proof that we should still follow the literal Ten Commandments just as the Israelites did. However, if you've read through the New Testament, you've probably also read many scriptures referring to the Law, Old Covenant, and Ten Commandments as already being fulfilled, made obsolete, nullified, passed away, and that we're no longer under the condemning authority of the law. Here are just a few examples of such texts:

14 having canceled out the certificate of debt consisting of decrees against us, which was hostile to us; and He has taken it out of the way, having nailed it to the cross. 15 When He had disarmed the rulers and authorities, He made a public display of them, having triumphed over them through Him 16 Therefore no one is to act as your judge in regard to food or drink or in respect to a festival or a new moon or a Sabbath day— 17 things which are a mere shadow of what is to come; but the substance belongs to Christ. Colossians 2:14-17 NASB.

> ...Truly, if there was a law that we could keep which would give us new life, then our salvation would have come by law-keeping. 22 But the Scriptures make it clear that since we were all under the power of sin, we needed Jesus. Galatians 3:21,22 TPT.

> [16] we know full well that we don't receive God's perfect righteousness as a reward for keeping the law, but by the faith of Jesus, the Messiah. Galatians 2:16 TPT.

> [10] But if you choose to live in bondage under the legalistic rule of religion, you live under the *law's curse*. For it is clearly written: "Utterly cursed is everyone who fails to practice every detail and requirement that is written in this law."[11] *For the Scriptures reveal,* and it is obvious, that no one achieves the righteousness of God by attempting to keep the law, for it is written: "Those who have been made holy will live by faith."[12] But keeping the law does not require faith, *but self-effort*. For the law teaches, "If you practice the principles of law, you must follow all of them."[13] Yet, Christ paid the full price to set us free from the *curse of the law*. He absorbed it completely as *He became a curse in our place...* Galatians 3:10-12.

My defense against such scriptures would have been, "Yeah, but these scriptures are only referring to all the ceremonial and festival laws, not the Ten Commandments written on stone..." But if you study it out for yourself, you'll find that *Scripture does not differentiate any higher or lesser importance between the Ten Commandments and the sanctuary instructions and rituals which were given to Moses on Mount Sanai at the same time*. In fact, all throughout scripture the law is most often referring to *everything* that was given to Moses that night, not just the Ten Commandments. (Jewish culture and history has always believed the "Law" equals all the instructions given to Moses that night, without isolated separation or exclusions) That consisted of the entire sanctuary construction directions/rituals, the items that were to be put inside of each compartment (including the Ten Commandments), which all pointed to various aspects of the Gospel of Jesus, who would be the actual fulfillment of what all those symbols represented. Trying to separate any part of the sanctuary or the items inside, would be to remove it out of its context. We'll see this clearer as we study this further.

For when *every commandment* had been spoken by Moses to all the people according to *the Law,* he took the blood of the calves and the goats, with water and scarlet wool and hyssop, and sprinkled both the book itself and all the people, [20] saying, "THIS IS THE BLOOD OF THE COVENANT WHICH GOD COMMANDED YOU." [21] And in the same way he sprinkled both the tabernacle and all the vessels of the ministry with the blood. Hebrews 9:19-21.

Notice "the covenant which God commanded you" consisted of the Ten Commandments *and* all of the sanctuary services.

Notice the following scriptures, which show the Old Covenant and Ten Commandments mingled as one; not separate or differentiated by any means:

> So he was there with the LORD forty days and forty nights; he did not eat bread or drink water. And he wrote on the tablets the *words of the covenant, the Ten Commandments.*" Ex 34:8 NASB.

> So He declared to you *His covenant* which He commanded you to perform, that is, *the Ten Commandments*; and He wrote them on two tablets of stone. Deut 4:13 NASB.

> It came about at the end of forty days and nights that the LORD gave me *the two tablets of stone, the tablets of the covenant.* Deut 9:11 NASB.

See also Deut. 9:9, 9:15, 1Kings 8:9,21

With this understanding of the 10 Commandments being the very "words of the covenant," verses like Hebrews 8:14 cannot be denied:

"When He said, "A new *covenant*," He has made the *first obsolete*. But whatever is becoming obsolete and growing old is ready to disappear."

I challenge you to reread the book of Hebrews, especially chapters 7-10 with this understanding, and see how clear the writer is to distinguish the differences of the Old and New Covenant laws and the experience of the believer. In the book of Galatians, you'll also see how vitally important it is not to get entangled into religiosity, and how getting entangled nullifies the true liberating Gospel of Jesus.

The more I studied how and when the word law is used throughout scripture, the more I started to realize that the separation of the Ten

Commandments and ceremony laws that I had believed, was actually *from Adventist theology, rather than Scripture.* But why would such a theology ever be brought into our beliefs? Because there's no other way to avoid the abundant Scriptures in the New Testament which refer to the Law/Old Covenant as being a "curse, ministry of death and condemnation, nullified, and obsolete."

So, *creating* a theological separation allows a person or denomination to decide which New Testament scriptures they want to apply to the Ten Commandments or not. I realized that's exactly what I had been doing, genuinely believing it to be true. But when God gave the sanctuary instructions, sacrificial Levitical protocols, and Ten Commandments, there was no separation or magnification. The *combined purpose* was to connect with sinful humanity. Each of these things represented different aspects of our salvation through the coming Savior, Jesus. I know we touched on Gal. 3:21 earlier, but now also read verses 21-25 together in the NKJV:

For if there had been a law given which could have given life, truly righteousness would have been by the law. ²²But the Scripture has confined all under sin, that the *promise by faith in Jesus* Christ might be given to those who believe. ²³But before faith came, we were kept under guard by the *law*, kept for the faith which would *afterward* be revealed. ²⁴Therefore the *law* was our tutor *to bring us* to Christ, that we might be justified by faith. ²⁵But after faith has come, we are no longer under a tutor. (Emphasis mine)

> We touched briefly on Heb. 8:13, but read the verses up to 9:7 for further clarity in the passion translation. (Keep in mind this passage is just after he described the New Covenant in chapter 8.)

This proves that, by establishing this New Covenant, the first is now obsolete, ready to expire, and about to disappear. Now, in the first covenant, there were specific rules for worship, including a sanctuary on earth to worship in.

²When you entered the tabernacle you would first come into the holy chamber where you would find the lampstand and the bread of his presence on the fellowship table. ³Then as you pass through the next curtain you would enter the innermost chamber called, the holiest sanctuary of all. ⁴It contained the golden altar of incense

and the ark of covenant mercy, which was a wooden box covered entirely with gold. And placed inside the ark of covenant mercy was the golden jar with mystery-manna inside, Aaron's resurrection rod, which had sprouted, and the *stone tablets engraved with the covenant laws.* [5] On top of the lid of the ark were two cherubim, angels of splendor, with outstretched wings overshadowing the throne of mercy. But now is not the time to discuss further the significant details of these things.[6] So with this *prescribed pattern of worship* the priests would routinely go in and out of the first chamber to perform their religious duties. [7] And the high priest was permitted to enter into the Holiest Sanctuary of All only once a year and he could never enter without first offering sacrificial blood for both his own sins and for the sins of the people.

The combination of everything Moses received from God that night on Mount Sanai is referred to here as a "prescribed pattern of worship."

Beginning from the outer court of the sanctuary were symbols and rituals pointing to the cleansing blood of Jesus. As the priest would perform these rituals and symbols on behalf of the people, he would physically advance closer and closer towards the final compartment of the Sanctuary (the most holy place), which is where the tangible presence of God was. But only once a year, on the Day of Atonement, could the high priest access this compartment *if* he correctly followed the prescribed pattern of worship from start to finish throughout the year. One mistake would literally cost him his life. In the Most Holy Place was the Arc of the Covenant, which represented the throne and presence of God. Inside of it were the tablets of the covenant/commandments, the golden pot that had manna, and Aaron's rod that budded.

Hebrews 9:8, 13 continues.

> Now the Holy Spirit uses the symbols of this pattern of worship to reveal that the perfect way of *holiness had not yet been unveiled*. For as long as the tabernacle stood [9] it was an illustration *that pointed to our present time of fulfillment*, demonstrating that offerings and animal sacrifices had *failed* to perfectly cleanse the conscience of the worshiper. [10] For this old pattern of worship was a matter of external rules

and rituals concerning food and drink and ceremonial washings which was imposed upon us *until* the appointed time of *heart-restoration* had arrived...[13] Under the old covenant the blood of bulls, goats, and the ashes of a heifer were sprinkled on those who were defiled and effectively cleansed them *outwardly* from their ceremonial impurities. [14] Yet how much more will the sacred blood of the Messiah thoroughly cleanse *our consciences.* For by the *power of the eternal Spirit* He has offered himself to God as the perfect Sacrifice that *now frees us from our dead works to worship and serve the living God.*

I once feared that by saying the "Old Covenant/Ten Commandments" are obsolete, meant we are promoting immoral lawlessness and a cheap grace. This fear is very common in Adventist theology, especially when we believe the majority of other Christians are already lawless if they don't follow the fourth commandment. But I only feared this because my understanding of holiness was the keeping of the Ten Commandment law. Hence, why I felt anything challenging its authority was deception.

This was until I started to see and understand the superior realm of holiness described in this passage. For example, in the Old Covenant *pattern of worship,* in which the Ten Commandments were given, "Worship was a matter of external rules and rituals." It was, in essence, powerless religion. That "prescribed pattern of worship" didn't remove even one sin from the people. It had no power to actually change the *conscience or heart* of the believer, as mentioned in the above passage. The Ten Commandment standard focused on the externals such as don't "murder, steal, etc."

The Pharisees easily kept the Ten Commandments and sanctuary rituals, and believed they were righteous because of it. But Jesus challenged their standard of holiness compared to the superior standard He was presenting. He said in Mat. 5:27-28, "Your ancestors have been taught, 'Never commit adultery.'[28] However, I say to you, if you look with lust in your eyes at the body of a woman who is not your wife, you've already committed adultery *in your heart.*" He elaborated the same way on the commandment of "do not murder," as well in vs. 21-22. Right before He started to describe this new covenant superior standard of Holiness regarding adultery and murder, He said in the previous verses 17-18:

> If you think I've come to set aside the law of Moses or the writings of the prophets, you're mistaken. I have come to *fulfill* and *bring to perfection all that has been written.* ¹⁸ Indeed, I assure you, as long as heaven and earth endure, not even the smallest detail of the Law will be done away with *until* its purpose is *complete.*

> When Hebrews is contrasted between the Old Covenant through Moses and the New Covenant in Christ, we see the *complete purpose* Christ talked about fulfilling in this text. For example, when we looked at Hebrews 9, verse 10 stated:

¹⁰ For this old pattern of worship was a matter of *external rules* and rituals concerning food and drink and *ceremonial washings* which was imposed upon us until the appointed time of *heart-restoration* had arrived.

In Chapter 3, we touched on the major differences between the Old vs. New Covenants. The heart vs. external performance is touched on in this paragraph from Chapter 3:

"In the Old covenant, man's closest understanding and practical experience of purity, holiness, and sanctification, was limited to the mere *external* disciplining and abstaining of one's *physical self or body* from sin. That's why, if you read the Old Testament books, specifically Exodus, Deuteronomy, and Leviticus, there is a heavy emphasis on the *external abstaining* from sin or "things unclean." The abstaining from kept the people very sin conscious, as this was *how* they were instructed to remain clean. Jesus hadn't died yet, our sins not legally forgiven, and therefore, we were unable to house the presence of the living God inside of us. So, without His indwelling presence, man functioned through many sacrificial, ceremonial, and traditional activity to *signify* the cleansing of their sin in the Old Testament, although *there was no actual transformation taking place.* This verse touches on that very point: "But in those *sacrifices there is* a reminder of sins every year. ⁴ For *it is not possible that the blood of bulls and goats could take away sins."* -Hebrews 10:3,4 NKJV. In other words, they were carrying out an *activity that was actually powerless to change them.* An intellectual acknowledgement of one thing while leaving the *practical life completely unaltered.* This is as far as man can operate apart from the indwelling presence of God – sin conscious, year after year, always shamed, guilty, defeated by the *big bad wolf,* the devil, while *intellectually and theologically* acknowledging certain teachings and carrying out certain religious traditions *apart* from true victory, transformation, freedom, of the indwelling presence of God."

In Chapters 7 and 8, we learned about the New Covenant birth of our regenerated inner man/spirit, and union with God's Holy Spirit, and how this union is far superior than any previous external laws and regulations in the Old Covenant. When we understand the superior realities of holiness from the inside out that the Gospel has now given us, we no longer fight to defend the old external ways of the Old Covenant.

God invites us into a true cleansing of our hearts and conscience, a transformation of our characters, not just our theology. He invites us to exchange our religious trophies of our efforts and obedience for His indwelling presence. He invites us out of the Old Covenant performance driven status of a *slave* and into the New Covenant status of a spiritual son/daughter of God. *It's not that Jesus' death changed the Ten Commandments, but it changed our experience of them from mere external applications (Old Covenant) into spiritual realities in Christ (New Covenant).*

As I kept seeking God out on this topic, I thought to myself, "Yeah, but what about Scriptures that speak about "keeping His commandments"?

Coming from a very law-emphasized religion, I genuinely believed that any Scripture that said "commandments," was yet another confirmation of how the Ten Commandments were being emphasized above all other forms. But what I failed to acknowledge was how often that word is used in the original language to mean commands or instruction, rather than always a reference to the physical law Ten Commandments. Hence, why more accurate translations of Scripture reflect the synonymous use. Here are a few examples of the word "commandments" used, even *before* the Ten Commandments were even given.

"Because that Abraham *obeyed my voice*, and kept my charge, my *commandments*, my statutes, and my laws." Gen 26:5 KJV.

And said, If thou wilt diligently *hearken to the voice of the LORD* thy God, and wilt do that which is right in his sight, and wilt give ear to his *commandments*, and keep all his statutes, I will put none of these diseases upon thee, which I have brought upon the Egyptians: for I am the LORD that healeth thee. Ex 15:26 KJV.

And the LORD said unto Moses, How long refuse ye to keep my *commandments* and my laws? Ex 16:28 KJV.

The term "commandments" was used in these accounts of Scripture *before* the introduction of the physical Ten Commandments given on Sinai. In fact, its reference in the above verses is synonymous with *obeying the voice of God*. It's used referring to the present instruction/commandments God had given to Abraham. Even before the tablets of stone, God had commandments regarding how He wanted the people to worship/sacrifice and behave. We see even from Genesis many commandments/commands God gave for the people to obey. But always with the same intent: connecting with His people. Prior to the physical Ten Commandments law, given on Sinai and even long after in the book of Revelation, this term, *commandments,* often refers to being obedient to what God IS saying, instead of only what He ONCE said on Mt. Sinai. It's actually much easier to say, "keep the Ten Commandments" than it is to say, "We need to be hearing (present tense) what Jesus is saying (present tense) so that we are following Him (present tense).

In the Scriptures above, note how "obeying His voice/hearkening the voice of the Lord precedes "giving ear to His commandments." It's no wonder Jesus said: "My sheep hear My voice, and I know them, and they follow Me;" Jn 10:27 NASB.

He could have said, "My sheep know my scriptures" or "my sheep know my law" but that's not what He says. It's always been about hearing His voice, knowing Him personally, and following Him. This "following Him" requires a present-hearing of His voice and experiencing (knowing) of His presence. It's why Jesus often said, "I only say what I hear My Father say and only do what I see Him do." The true followers of Jesus, His disciples, did exactly that, as they surrendered up their previous methods of work, to actually do life with Jesus on a daily basis.

But those who supposedly "kept the law" continued to maintain their religious forms, all while crucifying the present-speaking and doing of God displayed in Christ. They maintained faithful to their synagogue services and rituals while rejecting the embodiment of God's presence and voice in Jesus. The verse, "If you love Me you'll keep my commandments" takes on a much deeper meaning beyond the physical Ten Commandments, when we see it in its true context of New Testament reality. The Pharisees had no problem with the Ten Commandments written on stone but they were disgusted with Jesus' commandments and instruction in His teachings. To them, it seemed to undermine the Old Covenant they *faithfully* protected and followed. But had they been following God's voice instead, they would have heard its familiarity in the very words of Jesus.

Which of these two examples requires a deeper surrender of ourselves? 1. God I'm ready and willing to follow your command (present tense)? **OR,** 2. I'll follow the Ten Commandments?

I know, throughout my life growing up, there were many times I was following the Ten Commandments but lived far from following Jesus. To follow a list of external Ten Commandments can be done without any personal relationship with God. But surrendering to His every command, on a daily basis, is impossible without a relationship with Him. Again, the Pharisees followed the "Law" of the covenant while demanding the murder of Jesus. The disciples followed the presence of Jesus and listened to His everyday commands, and genuinely knew the living God, as a result.

Hebrews Chapter 1 mentioned that, in the Old Covenant era, God's voice was only heard by the prophets of old and, like Moses, they would convey what commandments God was saying unto the rest of the people. Then the people would merely attempt to carry out commandments of God, without ever *personally* hearing His voice.

Unfortunately, I've seen that same pattern repeated in any religious organization or people that follow Old Covenant methods. *It's a big mistake to put our trust in any man, woman or organization to hear God for us. When we do, we submit ourselves back into the slave/servant relationship that so many scriptures use to describe the Old Covenant era.* It cheats Christ out of the vibrant and supernatural relationship He died to bring us each into on a very intimate and personal level, Spirit to spirit.

From personal experience, I can tell you that Old Covenant religion can only take you so far. Many religious people are no longer "in Egypt," in the sense that they don't smoke, drink, etc., like they once did, but have they entered into a "spiritual Canaan?" How many times did the Israelites tell Moses, "You speak to God and find out what He wants us to do and we'll just do whatever He tells us to."? Their actions and words displayed they truly just wanted to find out, "What do we have to DO to keep God from being angry at us?" Like many today, "What do I need to DO so I don't go to hell?" They made it out of Egypt, but not into Canaan. Most spiritual dysfunction we see around us and, perhaps in us today, is often rooted in the same kind of unbelief.

Are we experiencing the supernatural kingdom that Jesus said is presently "at hand?" The supernatural power and presence of God? Or are we rejecting the true power and completion of the gospel of Jesus Christ, and exchanging it for powerless forms and traditions?

The book of Acts shares testimony after testimony of what the church resembles when we truly believe and experience New Covenant realities and intimacy with the living God. Apart from hearing His voice, there is no intimacy, or *knowing* Him, as Jn 10:27 said. Jesus said, "And this is life eternal, that they may know thee, the only true God and Jesus Christ whom you have sent." Jn 17:3. The Greek word for *know* here, isn't a mere intellectual acknowledgment of information, but to *experientially* know. It's in the personal hearing of God's voice, the perceiving of His presence and ways, that we experience the New Covenant realities of "knowing Him" beyond being mere servants/slaves in His house, but as sons and daughters of the living God. The priests and prophets of the Old Covenant era were mere glimpses of the New Covenant believer, and the access that the death of Christ would give us. God wants you to learn His supernatural ways and hear His voice for yourself. Thanks to Jesus, *you are already qualified to.*

I invite you to pray this prayer out loud:

Father, help me to hear Your voice more clearly. Help me to truly believe and receive the Gospel and all of the realities now available to me. Help me to surrender any parts of my heart, traditions, and life that have kept me away from Your presence.

In Jesus' name, Amen.

CHAPTER 17

RELIGIOUS MEDIATORS VS. JESUS

S ince Adam and Eve first sinned, humanity has had this empty void in our hearts only God Himself can fill. If we look back to the time of God's people, in the book of 1 Samuel, we see the people begging God to give them a king just like the other surrounding nations had. (1 Samuel 8:5-7). But their request was actually a rejection of God Himself being their King. He was the one who had provided for them and would lead them through various battles, but they insisted on a man instead. If you follow their story after this point, you will see the natural consequences of what happens when our faith and trust is in a human mediator rather than in God Himself. Cambridge online English dictionary defines *mediator* as a *"person who tries to end a disagreement by helping the two sides to talk about and agree on a solution."*

Despite Adam and Eve's mistake being the reason sin is in the world today, God has never stopped seeking to bring us back into unity and right relationship with Him <u>directly</u>. But even from the time of Moses (in the book of Exodus), the people wanted Moses to be their mediator, and for him to hear from God *for* them. Also, all of the priest protocols and sanctuary services of the Old Testament consisted of a man mediating between God and His children. In that scenario, the priest was a representation of Jesus who would one day come as the only true qualified mediator. Although the priest symbolically represented Jesus, he could not bring any true transformation, forgiveness, or permanent restoration between God and His children. Only Jesus would be able to do that.

[5] For there is one God, and *one mediator* also between God and men, *the* man Christ Jesus. 1 Timothy 2:5 NASB.

If God had sent Jesus as a permanent priest and prophet for His people, in the same way that the Old Testament structure was, it would have been better than any previous human priest or prophet. But God didn't send Jesus to merely mediate as an Old Covenant priest would. He sent Him to die for us so that the sin problem causing this separation between God and man could be done away with. In other words, His death actually removed the problem that caused a need for mediation in the first place. Romans 5:10 says that, "while we were yet enemies of God, we *were* reconciled (brought back to full divine favor) back to God through the death of His Son."

[14] Seeing then that we have a great High Priest who has passed through the heavens, Jesus the Son of God, let us hold fast *our* confession...[16] Let *us* therefore come *boldly* to the throne of grace, that we may obtain mercy and find grace to help in time of need. Hebrews 4:14,16 NKJV.

Just as in today's culture, a son wouldn't hesitate to approach his dad for anything, so we have been brought back into the family of God as His sons and daughters to have such incredible access once again. Sometimes, in the church there are theologies circulating of an angry God the Father and a kind Son Jesus who defends us (Usually because of certain Scriptures taken out of context). But Scripture says, "God (the Father) so LOVED the world that HE gave His son..." (Jn 3:16) (See also 2 Cor.5:19). God the Father, Jesus the Son, and Holy Spirit all wanted this union of God and man once again. Each of them had a vital part to play in this process.

The Father was the one who *sent* the Son, the Son the one who *died*, and the Holy Spirit was then sent to *live* inside of us as a result of the plan being complete and effective.

As we've learned from previous chapters, we are now "one spirit with Him" (1Cor.6:17). But when we still try to put our faith or trust in another human mediator to hear God *for us,* like in the Old Testament model prior to the cross, we are denying the truth of the Gospel, which has given us the legal right to approach God's throne with *boldness* as redeemed spiritual sons and daughters of God.

A lack of understanding or believing God's intent for us on a personal, direct, intimate level, results in us being vulnerable to man-made mediators once again. If you study various church histories over the last 100-200 years, you'll find various denominations and groups that fell into such a mistake. As a result, you'll see the exact same patterns of the Old Testament repeated, as the people following such an organization rely on human mediators to hear from

RELIGIOUS MEDIATORS VS. JESUS

God for them, rather than believing God has invited them to come to Him themselves. The pope and priests in the Catholic Church often propose their role as a mediator between church members and God. The Church of Latter Day Saints believed their prophet Joseph Smith heard a unique message directly from an angelic encounter. This "message" is recorded in the book of Mormon today. As a result, their members have unique isolated beliefs compared to most of Christendom, since they are rooted heavily in Joseph Smith's isolated and exclusive revelation. Jehovah's Witnesses also have very similar patterns in their origin and many isolated conclusions too.

The more I learned of my heavenly Father's love for me, and grew in my relationship with the Holy Spirit, the more I wondered if I had vulnerably fell into the same trap in my Adventist upbringing. Had I put more trust and faith in the writings and prophetic authority of one of our key founders, Ellen G. White, more than the Holy Spirit? As a Seventh Day Adventist, one of the doctrines you accept when getting baptized into the church is number 18 (of 28 doctrines) which says:

> "The Scriptures testify that one of the gifts of the Holy Spirit is prophecy. This gift is an identifying mark of the remnant church and we believe it **was** manifested in the ministry of Ellen G. White. Her writings speak with <u>prophetic</u> <u>authority</u> and provide comfort, guidance, instruction, and correction to the church. They also make clear that the Bible is the standard by which all teaching and experience must be tested." Copyright © 2015, General Conference of Seventh-day Adventists www.adventist.org (My emphasis)

Notice it says the gift of prophecy *was (*as in past tense), manifested through Ellen G. White. It doesn't say "one of the ways we've seen it manifest," (therefore believing God can still speak prophetically through people today), but instead *He already spoke this way through her.* Notice it also magnifies the gift of prophecy above the other gifts of the Spirit by saying, "This gift (of prophecy) is an *identifying mark of the remnant church...*" But Scripture never puts such magnification on prophecy over the other gifts of the Holy Spirit, nor does it say the gift of prophecy is "an identifying mark of the remnant church." Instead, Scripture says it's *one* of the gifts of the Holy Spirit.

For us to believe in such exclusive, isolated revelation and authority, instantly creates a mediator scenario once again. "Tell us what God is saying *for us*," is the position it puts the people of God back in. Scripture does "testify that one of the gifts of the Holy Spirit is prophecy" but it never says it is *exclusive* to any *one* particular *individual* or *denomination* isolated from any other Christian believers. Scripture never says the prophetic has an expiration date as though such divine revelation has ended. There is no Scripture in the New Testament that supports a fall back into the Old Testament mentality of "God _once_ said..." rather than "This is what the Lord _is_ saying today."

It's no wonder why I believed we *already* had all of the revelation God had to share for His people and needed nothing more. Such a belief isolates us into believing we have superior insight, compared to all of the other Christians around us. It creates a *religious pride of self-righteousness* that hinders our personal ability to hear God's present speaking today. It's this very mistake that is at the root of several of the "unique" doctrines of Adventism, such as the seventh day Sabbath, seal of the last day remnant (covered in Chapters 13-16), and several others we'll cover in this chapter.

However, when we start to believe God can and will speak to and through us personally and even in prophetic ways, it is incredible the kinds of things He loves to share with us and even for the strangers in front of us. The Bible teaches the supernatural gifts of the Holy Spirit are available to *all* believers and reveal the love and heart of God in supernatural ways before an unbelieving world. We'll touch more on this later.

Early on in my journey, when I was about eighteen years old, I became a diligent student of Ellen G. White's writings. Many things she wrote blessed me at the time. But much of her emphasis and interpretation of Scripture was greatly influencing how I would interpret Scriptures in order to support my Adventist belief. I had all of her writings, not only in digital format, but a good amount in physical form, too, which I studied, highlighted, and often quoted. In addition to her writings, I had the full Seventh-day Adventist Bible Commentary set in my home library, which I often referred to in my study of Scripture. I was well equipped to share why we believed what we did.

As I worked for various SDA churches and conferences (Florida conf., Georgia conf., and Texas conf.) over the years, I realized how many church leaders, pastors, and even SDA theologians lacked in their own knowledge and study of these resources. This was also evident by how different the culture of Adventism would vary in different churches in different regions. I'd find some more legalistic than others, some believed Ellen White's writings, while others didn't, and some were more liberal than others. I not only believed in so much of what she wrote, but even spent several years distributing her books as a Magabook student and, eventually, a Magabook leader (in GA. and FL.). In the years that followed, I researched and studied what many critics had written against her in various documents and defended them while feeling secure in the belief I had in her authenticity as a prophetess of God.

With that background, it's no wonder why the Holy Spirit showed me things from personally experiencing the scriptures *first* and then took me back to examine Adventist history and the authenticity of Ellen G. White, rather than the other way around.

ADVENTIST HISTORY IN THE 1800-1900 ERA VS. CHRISTIAN HISTORY

With all of my study of our church history, I genuinely believed what we had documented in the "Advent movement" was much greater than any other church's history during the 1800-1900 era. Yet, in my spiritual journey more recently, I've learned of many other resources that have recorded revivals of *much greater* Biblical proportion and witnesses, not just from Christian resources, but secular newspapers and media during the same century.

Charles Finney (Born 1791). One of my favorite stories about Charles Finney is when he was prayerfully walking through a cotton mill full of workers. Without saying a word, the presence of God overflowing from him began to convict one of the workers who had actually mocked the work of God through Finney. She was overwhelmed to the point of trembling and tears and repented of her sins that very moment, although he hadn't said a word to her. This presence of God then began to spread all over the factory like a domino effect, which caused the owner of the mill to come out and see what was happening. He was so deeply moved by what he was seeing the presence of God do, that he stopped the mill and said it was more important that all of their souls be saved than for the mill to run. Several reports say that nearly every one of the employees were saved and a revival of more than 3,000 people was the result. This is just one of such revival accounts from Finney's ministry.

Maria Woodworth-Etter (Born 1844). Reports state within days of her coming to a town after sleeping in a tent there would be approximately 20,000 people in her meetings. At times, as people would be working in the fields within a fifty-mile radius from her meetings and God would give them visions of heaven and hell, and they would fall to the ground under tremendous conviction. It was like a "blanket" anointing of God's presence that would come down upon the whole area. Reports say that even for whole blocks around her meetings, people would be falling to the ground and repenting.

Smith Wigglesworth (Born 1859). His only training was as a plumber. He encountered the Holy Spirit and became a fiery preacher and minister of the Gospel. He had a powerful healing ministry across numerous countries, which included the healing of many tumors, cancers, tuberculosis, wheelchair-bound diseases and afflictions, demon possessions, and many other conditions. Accounts say trucks would have to remove the many wheelchairs and crutches from his meetings due to the miraculous healings. Several accounts speak of pastors who joined him for prayer meeting and, once he started praying, the presence of God would overwhelm the place to the point that the pastors one by one felt forced to leave in fear of it killing them.

John G. Lake (Born 1870.) God sent him to Africa where his anointed miracle ministry was described as the most extensive and powerful missionary movement in all Africa. He then came back to America to Spokane, Washington, which resulted in no less than 100,000 astounding miracles of healing within the space of five or six years. Several secular news sources affirmed the incredible change of health in the city due to the power of God abiding there. The fruits of this ministry continue to be one of the most credible documented sources of countless divine healings. This ministry, www.Jglm.org still trains believers to heal the sick according to the Biblical redeemed status of sons/daughters of God filled with the Holy Spirit. (One of such trainings is available online and in person titled, "Divine Healing Technician Training" (DHT) by Curry Blake. The content of that training has blessed me greatly as its truths have broken off many other Old Covenant mindsets I had regarding healing for today etc.)

A book that has put together many of these spiritual revivalists along with other recorded and researched accounts is, *God's Generals* by Roberts Liardon. While researching these moves of God, I was amazed to see the pattern of God's Spirit moving from one area of the globe to another, from one group of believers to the next, and see how that group stewarded His presence or not. I saw so many similarities, synonymous with the early church described in the book of Acts. In *God's Generals*, I especially liked that the author shared the good, bad, and ugly of each "General," which provokes one to want to avoid the same mistakes today.

As you read each of these movements of God in our recent history, you will find yourself saying, "God, I didn't know you were still this active today." In contrast, *when I used to study the history of Adventist pioneers as the only inspired history, I'd be provoked to put more faith into their spirituality and their ability to hear God more than mine.* I had this sense of, "Well, they were hearing God with visions and I'm not, so surely I can trust their word over what I may currently understand." But when I've studied *other* revivals and moves of God during that same era, I find myself believing more in God's ability to do the same in me today. There's such power in the testimony. When *His* works and *His* activity is testified, it creates faith in us and positions one to experience what is being testified for themselves. This continues to happen to me on this amazing journey with the Holy Spirit.

I believed Ellen G. White's ability to hear from God, experience visions, and write so many books, was enough credible proof that the Advent movement was started and continued by God. Yet, there are many conflicting areas of Adventist beliefs that we've merely scratched the surface on, and that show this movement was actually a move back into Old Covenant mindsets and beliefs, hence, the absence of God's endorsing supernatural power today in the church. Our history and much of present day Adventism displays a culture of, "Tell us what God is saying for us to do," just like the Israelites in the

Old Covenant. The only difference is the Israelites relied on Moses' ability to hear from God, whereas *much of Adventism has been built upon the pioneer's ability to hear from God, and, specifically, Ellen White's ability to hear from God.* There may be people even reading this book who will be prone to settle for *whatever* responses their pastor or conference officials say regarding these points. Sometimes, we may mistakenly put more faith in our local church leaders, pastors, and elders as mediators rather than in the Holy Spirit. But I pray instead, our discussion causes you to grow more intimately with the Holy Spirit and that you will prioritize His voice over anyone else's man made title or authority. It's His voice alone that gives us life and a deeper hunger for more of Him. It's Him alone that pulls us into the New Covenant reality in real life, not mere theology.

What is scary to me is how many times in Adventist history, E.G.W. was the <u>only one</u> endorsing a particular belief and how many people back then and now put their faith in her *exclusive* revelation, despite its contradiction of scripture. As God started to challenge my "faith" in her divine authority, I started to see numerous examples in writings that were contradicting to scripture and shouldn't be ignored. In Chapters 13-16, we covered her isolated vision of the seventh day Sabbath, the isolated teaching of the end times seal, and magnification of the physical Ten Commandments, compared to New Covenant realities and truths. In our next chapter, we will cover a few more examples.

CHAPTER 18

SCRIPTURE EXPOSES THE LIE

A dventist belief teaches when Jesus ascended into heaven, He only entered into the first compartment of the heavenly sanctuary, called the "Holy place" and remained there until 1844, when He moved into the second compartment called, the "Most Holy place," where He began the "Investigative Judgement." (see *The Great Controversy,* p.421; *Early Writings* p.251; *Spiritual Gifts* vol.1 p.159).

In other words, Jesus simply became a mediator just like the Old Covenant model and was gradually making His way to the Most Holy place in a *physical sanctuary* just like the earthy sanctuary in the Old Testament. However, the earthly tabernacle was physically symbolic of the redemptive ways Jesus earthly life and death would bring us into the presence and throne room of God. Each thing they had been instructed to put in that earthly tabernacle (table of show-bread, candle stick menorah, etc.) pointed forward to Jesus, who would be the reality of the symbol (Jesus became the "bread of life" and "light of the world"). Hebrews 9:11,12 (we'll read below) is clear that in heaven, the tabernacle is *"not made with hands, that is, not of this creation,"* and therefore, not a physical layout like the earthly one which was given for symbolic purposes. The Scripture below is also clear that Jesus entered "the Most Holy Place" once and for all, namely the very throne room of God, not a physical compartment of a symbolic structure that He remained for decades.

As we continue, you'll find the Adventist "belief" of Jesus ascending into an inferior physical compartment rather than the actual presence of God's throne, is subduing a liberating Gospel reality back into an Old Covenant era of time.

As we also discussed last chapter, Jesus' priestly ministry was entirely different being that it was the shedding of *His* blood that mediated in our behalf, and forgave our sins to bring us back (reconcile) us back to the Father. No priestly rituals or symbolisms would be necessary from the Old Covenant since His blood actually *did* change the sin problem unlike the symbolic lamb's blood.

Hebrews 9:11-15 (NKJV) says:

11 But Christ came as High Priest of the good things to come, with the greater and more perfect tabernacle not made with hands, that is, not of this creation. 12 Not with the blood of goats and calves, but with His own blood He entered the Most Holy Place once for all, having obtained eternal redemption. 13 For if the blood of bulls and goats and the ashes of a heifer, sprinkling the unclean, sanctifies for the purifying of the flesh, 14 how much more shall the blood of Christ, who through the eternal Spirit offered Himself without spot to God, cleanse your conscience from dead works to serve the living God? 15 And for this reason He is the Mediator of the New Covenant, by means of death, for the redemption of the transgressions under the first covenant, that those who are called may receive the promise of the eternal inheritance.

Please note, Scripture clearly says His blood is the means in which "He entered (past tense) the MOST HOLY PLACE (throne room of God) once for all." Hebrews chapter 9 specifically contrasts the symbolic yet ineffective means of the earthly animal sacrifices and structure of the Old Covenant priests vs. Jesus' sacrifice of His blood. To say Jesus didn't actually go into the Most Holy place/throne room when He ascended into heaven is to deny the truth Hebrews so clearly emphasizes His blood gave us direct access to. The power of believing in that reality can actually "cleanse your conscience from dead works" not merely "purify your flesh" through physically abstaining from symbolic means like they did in the Old Covenant.

Like we discussed in Chapter 17, it goes beyond the external "do not kill" commandment and instead, "if you hate your brother you already committed murder" (Mat 5:21-22). The reality of true heart obedience that Jesus describes in that sermon, was not attainable in the Old Covenant, hence, why the Jews He was teaching this to were so perplexed. Rejecting the truth of Jesus' ascension into the Most Holy Place is unbelief and rejecting the complete Gospel truth as it is in Christ.

When I looked to hear what Adventist theologians said about this, I read articles of them trying to use the Greek as a means to explain away the point above, despite numerous Bible scholars of Greek New Testament and most Bible translations translating the about passage as "Most Holy Place." But even apart from the clear grammatical use of "Most Holy Place," contextually/theologically, the throne of God that we're invited to "come boldly" to in Heb. 4:16 was represented in the Most Holy place compartment in the Old Covenant Sanctuary, not in the Holy place compartment which preceded it. Several other scriptures also tell us exactly where Jesus ascended to when He went up to heaven:

> Now the point in what we are saying is this: we have such a high priest, one who is *seated at the right hand of the throne of the Majesty in heaven*... Hebrews 8:1

> After making purification for sins, he (Jesus) sat down *at the right hand of the Majesty on high*... -Hebrews 1:3.

> [2] But *when* Christ had offered for all time a single sacrifice for sins, He *sat down at the right hand of God*, Hebrews 10:12 (see also <u>Acts 7:55–56-The heavens open and Stephen sees Jesus standing at the right hand of God; Romans 8:34; Ephesians 1:20; Colossians 3:1</u>).

> In summary of this point, Scripture is very clear, Jesus' blood was truly a sufficient sacrifice that redeemed us right into the very throne room of our heavenly Father. Scripture *does not* support or teach the Adventist belief that Jesus ascended into a physical "holy place compartment" of a "heavenly sanctuary" and waited until 1844 before He moved into the "most holy place." This belief contradicts the Word of God and is an offense to the completed work of Jesus.

A TIME WITHOUT AN INTERCESSOR

I began to question other areas of Adventist theology that placed a non-scriptural emphasis or expiration date ("but when the end times come…") on certain aspects of the Gospel. These kinds of emphasis undermine the true gospel and complete atonement of Christ and cause a person's faith/belief to shift unto themselves rather than in Jesus. I found many of these non-Biblical emphases are very "fear driven."

Ellen G. White says in her book, *The Great Controversy* p. 425:

> *"Those who are living upon the earth when the <u>inter-cession of Christ shall cease</u> in the sanctuary above are to stand in the sight of a holy God without a mediator. Their robes must be spotless, their characters must be purified from sin by the blood of sprinkling. Through the grace of God and <u>their own diligent effort</u> they must be conquerors in the battle with evil. While the investigative judgment is going forward in heaven, while the sins of penitent believers are being removed from the sanctuary, there is to be a special work of purification, of putting away of sin, among God's people upon earth."*

> Will there ever be a church or body of believers on the earth that are truly "without spot or wrinkle?" Yes but *how* that is accomplished is the major difference between Old Covenant theology ("*by your own diligent effort*") versus New Covenant realities (His Spirit indwelling in us and through us). Despite how long other Adventists and I have clung to such claimed "prophecies" from Ellen White, the Bible *clearly* presents a *different* truth regarding Christ's intercession versus the Old Covenant priests:

> Hebrews 7:23-25

> [23] The *former* priests, on the one hand, existed in greater numbers because they were prevented by

death from continuing, ²⁴but Jesus, on the other hand, because He continues forever, holds His priesthood permanently. ²⁵Therefore He is able also to save forever those who draw near to God through Him, since He always lives to make intercession for them.

Regardless of "sin abounding" in the inconsistent world today, we can put full confidence, not half confidence or temporary confidence, until the end times come, but FULL CONFIDENCE in the intercession of Jesus because He *"holds His priesthood permanently"* and *"always lives to make intercession for us."* If you read all of Hebrews 7, this is sharply contrasted to the Old Covenant order and flaws, in which the priest couldn't actually atone for anyone's sins, (being that he was a sinner too) and couldn't offer a sufficient sacrifice other than the symbolic blood of goats/calves. Nowhere does Scripture place an "end time" condition on the intercession of Christ. Instead, it clearly declares His permanent intercession on our behalf. Anything less, causes us to doubt in the fullness of Jesus sacrifice and role as our intercessor, and place our trust/faith in our own diligent efforts of law keeping. Keep in mind the sanctuary type language used throughout this passage in Hebrews is written to Hebrew Jews who were struggling to accept Jesus as the fulfillment of everything they believed in the Old Covenant rituals and symbols.

CONFLICTING THEOLOGY AND VISIONS

As I've continued to look further into the process and steps that Adventist pioneers took to conclude some of the key doctrines of Adventism (The three angel's message interpretation, investigative judgement, Sabbath, law, etc.) I continued to see much contradiction of Scripture, the Gospel, and even of their own prior visions, which they had said were from God. I also saw how much effort had been *humanly done* to "keep everything intact."

One example of this includes how the Ellen White Estate changed/omitted parts of visions in her book "Early Writings," which supported the "shut door" theory that she eventually renounced (The older versions of *Early Writings* have the full vision, but the more modern versions leave out the part that emphasized the "shut door" teaching.)

You're probably wondering, "What is the shut door teaching and why would they try to cover that up?" I'll explain more below, but the reason we are touching on this is because the same way it came about (through an E.G.W exclusive vision), the way it was taught (believe it equals you're saved, rejecting equals you're lost) and the way it's been explained away over the years, all reveal a lack of Biblical origin, divine endorsement, and spiritual authority. It is also another example of the same exact pattern I saw when the pioneers "discovered" and taught the Sabbath doctrine, based on an exclusive E.G.W vision (Covered in Chapters 13-16).

This "shut door" teaching was the belief that once Jesus went into the "most holy place" (which according to Adventist was in 1844), probation for everyone else was closed and they were *lost* hence, the "shut door" belief. To be even more specific, it was taught that only those who had accepted the investigative judgment, Sabbath, 1844 teachings, and interpretation of the three angels' message as E.G.W. and the pioneers had believed, would be those whom made it "in" while the rest were lost.

Here is a quote from E.G.W., explaining from one of her "visions," how the Advent believers at the time were to believe in regard to those "outside" of the "shut door:"

> "I saw that Jesus prayed for his enemies, <u>but that should not cause us to pray for the wicked world, whom God had rejected</u>—when he prayed for his enemies, there was hope for them, and they could be benefited and saved by his prayers, and also after he was a mediator in the outer apartment for the whole world; but <u>now his spirit and sympathy were withdrawn from the world</u>; and our sympathy must be with Jesus, <u>and must be withdrawn from the</u>

ungodly. I saw that God loved his people—and, in answer to prayers, would send rain upon the just and the unjust—I saw that now, in this time, that he watered the earth and caused the sun to shine for the saints and the wicked by our prayers, by our Father sending rain upon the unjust, while he sent it upon the just. <u>I saw that the wicked could not be benefited by our prayers now</u>—and although he sent it upon the unjust, yet their day was coming. Then I saw concerning loving our neighbors. <u>I saw that scripture did not mean the wicked whom God had rejected that we must love</u>, but he meant our neighbors in the household, and <u>did not extend beyond the household</u>; yet I saw that we should not do the wicked around us any injustice:—but, <u>our neighbors whom we were to love, were those who loved God and were serving him</u>." Camden, N.Y., June 29, 1851 (See Canright, *The Life of Mrs. E.G.White, p.127*)

Ellen White not only believed, taught, and wrote about this for about nine or more years (as evidenced by her writings and teachings during this time) but as shown above, she even claimed God had given her specific visions (*"I saw"*) to endorse this as being from Him, and then later she denies they ever happened. This is seen in the following example, where in the context of the "shut door" belief she pens the following:

"I HEREBY TESTIFY in the fear of God that...With my brethren and sisters, after the time passed in forty-four I did believe no more sinners would be converted.

But I NEVER HAD A VISION that no more sinners would be converted. And am clear and free to state that no one has ever heard me say or has read from my pen statements which will justify them in the charges they have made against me upon this point.... I have ever had messages of reproof for those who used these harsh expressions." Selected Messages, Vol. 1, p. 74.

Shattering RELIGION'S HOLLOW SHELL

So here she denies ever having a vision about this, but both she and her husband wrote in other places that she *did* in fact have visions about this as you'll see in these quotes:

James White

When she received her first vision, Dec. 1844, she and all the band in Portland, Maine, [where her parents then resided] had given up the midnight-cry, and shut door, as being in the past. IT WAS THEN THAT THE LORD SHEW HER IN VISION, the error into which she and the band in Portland had fallen. She then related her vision to the band, and about sixty confessed their error, and acknowledged their seventh month experience to be the work of God" A Word to the Little Flock, 1847, p.22.

In that quote, her husband refers to a time when she and the other believers in Portland were doubting the shut door belief but then "the Lord shew her in vision" their error (of not believing it) and they confessed and acknowledged what they had been believing about the shut door for the last seven months was actually from "God." (According to her vision) She refers to an experience very similar if not the same as this, in this quote:

Ellen White

"The view about the Bridegroom's coming I had about the middle of February, 1845, while in Exeter, Maine, in meeting with Israel Dammon, James, and many others.

Many of them did not believe in a <u>shut door</u>. I suffered much at the commencement of the meeting. Unbelief seemed to be on every hand....There was one sister there that was called very spiritual. She had traveled and been a powerful preacher the most of the time for twenty years. She had been truly a mother in Israel. But a division had risen in the band on the shut

*door. She had great sympathy, and could not believe_*
the door was shut. I had known nothing of their dif-
ference. Sister Durben got up to talk. I felt very, very
sad... "At length my soul seemed to be in agony, and
while she was talking I fell from my chair to the floor.
It was then I had a view of Jesus rising from His medi-
atorial throne and going to the holiest as Bridegroom
to receive His kingdom. They were all deeply inter-
ested in the view. They all said it was entirely new to
them. The Lord worked in mighty power, setting the
truth home to their hearts....Most of them received
the vision, and were settled upon the shut door.

(Letter B-3-1847, Letter to Joseph Bates, July 13, 1847)

If you study further into the origins of any of the other unique key doctrines of Adventism, you'll find the same pattern noted in the examples of the "Shut door" and of the "seventh day Sabbath. At the introduction of these "doctrines" were "endorsing visions" from Ellen G. White who then magnified the importance of the doctrine with a clause like:

"I saw this truth as being the truth that separates God's true church from the false, and those who reject it will be deceived into utter darkness..."

I've seen in my life how that repetitive clause or warning from Ellen White would ring in my subconscious and of so many Adventist if we'd even think of exploring anything that could question what we have believed for so long. It's that fear of being "deceived" along with "the Sunday churches" that has created such a self-righteous, self-endorsing, and man-made separation of Adventism from the rest of Christianity.

SUPERNATURAL HEALING

"...For this purpose the Son of God was manifested, that he might destroy the works of the devil." 1 John 3:8 KJV

When we read the account of Jesus' life on the earth, you cannot separate His verbal messages and sermons from the *demonstrations* of supernatural power from heaven. It wasn't uncommon for an entire city to experience this power of God through Jesus, and be delivered from *all* of their sickness, diseases, and demonic power-"the works of the devil." But then He invites us to do the exact same thing by the same Holy Spirit power when He says,

⁷ And as you go, preach, saying, 'The kingdom of heaven ⁽ⁱˢ ᵃᵗ ʰᵃⁿᵈ.⁾ ⁸ Heal *the* sick, raise *the* dead, cleanse *the* lepers, cast out demons. Freely you received, freely give. Matthew 10:7-8 NASB

> "Go into all the world and preach the gospel to all creation. ¹⁶ He who has believed and has been baptized shall be saved; but he who has disbelieved shall be condemned. ¹⁷ *These signs will accompany those who have believed: in My name they will cast out demons, they will speak with new tongues; ¹⁸ they will pick up serpents, and if they drink any deadly poison, it will not hurt them; they will lay hands on the sick, and they will recover.* Mark 16:15-18 NASB.

The entire book of Acts records the early church receiving the promised Holy Spirit and then the supernatural lifestyle He has given us through His Spirit. We have no other model of the New Covenant other than this supernatural power of God destroying the works of the devil. *There is no Scripture stating this supernatural power and presence of God would "one day expire or decrease."* Instead, Scripture says it will increase. It is only in the Old Covenant belief system that we see a "form *without* power." But then why did I, along with many Adventist leaders, believe they had expired? Where does this idea of "expired supernatural fruits" come from? I believe it stemmed from the pioneers, as the below quote from E.G.W. reveals what they had concluded about the supernatural evidences of Holy Spirit in their day:

"The way in which Christ worked was to preach the Word, and to relieve suffering by miraculous works of healing. But <u>I am instructed that we cannot now work in this way</u> for Satan will exercise his power by working miracles. God's servants today could not work by means

of miracles, because spurious works of healing, claiming to be divine, will be wrought." 2SM 54 (1904).

> Such instruction is a clear contradiction to the power of the Gospel and the Holy Spirit's indwelling presence that Jesus clearly demonstrated and invited every disciple of *every era* into. I remember hearing popular Adventist ministers use many quotes like the one here, to claim:

"I don't need signs, wonders and miracles. I'm a mature Christian and therefore His written word is enough for me."

Despite that, I know that I and other Adventist had "tried" at some point in our life to pray for healing for someone and it didn't happen. Such a disappointment can make any of us more vulnerable to human rationalizations and theologies like I too had eventually believed. But I've learned now that we aren't to put our experiences of failure over the truth of scripture. For example, "Since it didn't work, then perhaps that Scripture about healing is conditional and the conditions are..." It's humanly easier to put the "blame" back on God or even the person's lack of faith instead of taking spiritual accountability for ourselves. Jesus' example doesn't show Him failing to heal anybody nor does His command for us to follow Him justify such rationalizations for our disappointments. So, we can either make up a false theology to exclude such scriptures from our own life or realize that we need to grow more and thank God for His patience with us in the meantime.

When my mindset and beliefs were in synch with what my Adventist church, pastors, fellow Adventist members, and Adventist pioneers believed, I had the same lack of breakthrough they did, if I even dared to pray for someone to be healed or delivered. Not one testimony or demonstration of God's endorsing presence and power. If these "signs follow them that believe" as Jesus says in Mat. 16:17, I had to eventually admit, "I must have missed something in what I am supposed to believe in." Much of what I eventually grew to understand about the New Covenant realities I have shared in this book. The more aligned with Scripture and the early church of Acts my beliefs have come, the more testimonies and supernatural experiences we continue to see. It is absolutely incredible believing and living life as a supernatural son of the living God and it's all thanks to the blood of Jesus and the presence of the Holy Spirit.

Like I mentioned earlier in the previous chapter, God used many revivals and leaders outside of Adventism during that same 1800-1900 era, who had many healings, signs, wonders, and miracles just as the early church did in Acts. It's in that context we find the Adventist pioneers trying to "explain" to their followers "why those things aren't happening with us." The result? Explanations and theology of unbiblical positions that worsened over time, a <u>human</u> emphasis of various "signs" they claimed distinguished themselves as God's "true church (seventh day Sabbath/Investigative judgment)," but the clear lack of God's supernatural endorsement of His power and presence. Hence, the Ellen White, "I've been shown..." explanations used by past and present ministers responding to such questioning.

There are quotes where E.G.W. says all of the other revivals happening outside of Adventism were "false revivals" (despite their fruit being consistent with New Testament Christianity whereas Adventism's wasn't). I saw how this same mindset effected myself and many fellow Adventist whenever outside supernatural testimonies were mentioned or discussed. I would want to warn others, *"Don't be deceived brother. Don't fall for the Sunday worshiper's false revivals."*

It's a religious false humility that is used to avoid the obvious lack of divine endorsement. The only type of fruit that mindset/belief has produced, is a return to the powerless Old Covenant system of symbolic form without power. It's offering people we visit in the hospital a "prayer of comfort" rather than a prayer that delivers supernatural healing. It's the belief that every bad thing you experience is "God's way of testing you" or "using you as a testimony" rather than recognizing the devil is solely responsible for your pain, and God wants us to be free from any and everything that is oppressing our life. Its living a defeated life in which "sin" and the "devil" are at large and we're simply "hanging on" until Jesus comes back to rescue us out of here rather than growing in our divine supernatural authority so that we destroy the works of the devil as Jesus has commanded us to. It's offering the world a powerless form-religion, instead of the Living Christ.

I've humanly made the same mistake trying to reason out why we didn't need to demonstrate or experience God's supernatural power or hear His voice. I've personally seen the kind of fruit or lack thereof adhering to those statements produces. It truly is a quenching of the Holy Spirit- not a superior enlightenment of Him.

In 1910 (just a few years after the non-Adventist Azusa street revival started in L.A California 1906 accompanied by an *abundance* of worldwide recognized signs, wonders, and miracles of God), she writes,

"We are not to receive the words of those who come with a message that contradicts the <u>special points </u>of our faith. They gather together a mass of Scripture, and pile it as proof around their asserted theories. This has been done over and over again during the past fifty years. And while the Scriptures are God's Word, and are to be respected, the application of them, if such application moves one pillar of the foundation that God has sustained these fifty years, is a great mistake. He who makes such an application knows not the wonderful demonstration of the Holy Spirit that gave power and force to the past messages that have come to the people of God." Call to the Watchman, p.20 Ellen G. White 1910.

Did you catch what she says here? Respect the word of God *until* or *unless* its application challenges one pillar of the foundation "God has sustained these fifty years..." I saw how the common culture of Adventism seemed to be "we already have all the light we need." But our beliefs, no matter how old, must be aligned and corrected more and more to scripture, and rejected if it contradicts it.

I saw that same mentality she expressed in that quote perpetuated in myself and in the culture of Adventism. Anytime I would come across a statement or scripture that seemed to contradict a particular Adventist doctrine I would go to an Adventist Commentary, E.G.W. writings, or a general conference resource, to hear their explanation so that I could use it to maintain the special points of our faith. They seemed to always have an explanation readily available for anything that would reveal any inconsistencies or contradictions in Adventism. Yet just as the endorsing visions of E.G.W were the origins of the seventh day Sabbath emphasis, rather than the mere study of scripture accompanied by the Holy Spirit, so many have exchanged the role of Holy Spirit for their church leadership's answers and explanations. But, Jesus never said He would leave us a conference leader, prophet, or Bible commentary to guide us into all truth. He said the Holy Spirit was the qualified and equipped guide into all truth.

"But when He, the Spirit of truth, comes, <u>He</u> will guide you into <u>all the truth</u>; for He will not speak on His own initiative, but whatever He hears, He will speak; and <u>He will disclose to you what is to come</u>. John 16:13.

> Despite these clear instructions in Scripture about Holy Spirit's role as our guide, the mentality I used to have was, "We always have an answer because we've had the truth and complete revelation all along, whereas everyone else doesn't."

"We have the truth and you don't" is the Pharisee-like position that is anything but the childlike attitude Jesus said is so vital to seeing the kingdom.

I've read numerous quotes from Ellen White in her book, *"The Great Controversy,* where she warns and even condemns listening to Adventist who have left the church and come back to share what God has shown them to be true. With such instruction, your only hope to prevent yourself from being deceived is make sure you don't listen, read, or watch anyone who doesn't believe as an Adventist, and listen exclusively to what Adventist say is okay to.

Over the years, I've heard numerous conference leaders and pastors instruct their members to abstain from *any* outside sermons and writings, in order to keep themselves from being deceived. This fear of being deceived is truly a big insecurity that shows the lack of true divine substance. <u>It's also extremely manipulative and models the exact patterns of an abusive relationship, in which only those on the outside can actually see the abuse, hence why the abuser demands exclusive attention to maintain the cycle of abuse.</u> That cycle is the same for physical, mental, emotional, and spiritual abuse.

However, it is very common of God to bring significant change from the inside out. Saul of tarsus who became Paul the apostle, is one example. A highly respected Pharisee whose encounter with the living Christ changed him into a person who would uproot the very core of Judaism's strongholds he once genuinely defended. He became the most prominent New Testament writer who explains the most vital details of the gospel of Jesus Christ. I believe it was in fear of that same possibility happening to Adventism that Ellen White makes sure to "warn" of a similar thing.

We've only scratched the surface regarding the mediation of E.G.W.'s prophetic role in the Adventist church. There are plenty of resources you can find that go much more in-depth with other concerning areas of her ministry and the Advent pioneers. (The majority of these resources are not from outside critics but written by people who *were* Adventist leaders/pastors, held high positions in the conference and/or Adventist Universities, etc.). But even just with what we've covered so far in this book, are teachings from her that completely undermine the gospel, mediation of Jesus, and contradict scripture. I wondered by me receiving such teachings as inspired truth for so long, had I subconsciously placed my faith/belief into the mediation of E.G.W.'s ministry and authority to hear God *for me*? Could this be why I and so many fellow believers didn't believe God wanted to speak to us personally in supernatural ways today? I felt God challenge my heart saying, "What fruit can the Advent movement truly point to that resonates with New Testament Christianity?" In what ways has this movement stewarded or rejected the spiritual inheritance and realities of the New Covenant as demonstrated in the church of Acts? How about the presence of God? So many of the religious practices and beliefs we hold near and dear have no place in the New Covenant experience, as we have identified in this book. Instead, it has far more resonation and oneness with the Old Covenant, hence it's lack of New Covenant fruit. I realized more and more that we have a highly prized monument built by Adventist pioneers and then perpetuated as the "truth we must protect from end time deceptions." I realized the very thing I fought so hard to defend and protect my whole life, was the very belief system quenching the active work the Holy Spirit desired to carry out in my life and the fellow believers around me.

As we covered in the previous chapter, each of us are born with a void in our hearts that only God can fill. This void can be a vulnerability to desire a human mediator to give us a security of our standing and relationship with God. But in reality, that security is false, as the only true qualified mediator is Jesus Christ Himself. As far as a guide, or helper, the Holy Spirit is God's gift to each of us *personally* and *individually* to function in this capacity (Jn.14:26). The more we spend time with Him, learn to hear His voice, and follow His ways, the clearer our beliefs become of who we are as God's children, and who our heavenly Father is. After all, "...it was to us that God revealed these things by his Spirit. For his Spirit searches out everything and shows us God's deep secrets." 1 Cor.2:10.

CHAPTER 19

HE INVITES YOU INTO THE MORE

As God continued to win my heart and character over to Him through a growing, supernatural, relationship with Holy Spirit, I wanted to maintain my focus on His presence everywhere I went no matter what I was doing. I wanted to find other believers whose hearts had also been deeply provoked to experience more of God's presence and ways. Holy Spirit will guide you to the right resources, relationships, and experiences at the right time. A quote once said, "If you want to go where you've never gone you have to be willing to do what you've never done."

I published one book before this called, Identity Crisis, in 2014. In it, I shared more external testimonies/fruit such as praying healing for people, words of knowledge for strangers, and other experiences I had started to experience during that time (It was not edited and is very rough, from a grammar perspective but the content was what was fresh on my heart then.) I shared in that book how I was provoked by hearing testimonies of healings today from various ministries and people like Todd White, Dan Mohler, Bill Johnson, Randy Clark, and many others at churches I'd begun to visit locally. What's so great about these types of experiences and everything we've been discussing in this book, is since its origin is from God Himself rather than a particular man/woman, it is 100% directly available to you. Hearing testimonies is needed to raise our level of expectancy and belief (especially if you have a lifetime of testimonies of unbelief), but what's even more exciting is when Holy Spirit leads you to putting it into action and seeing someone benefit in front of you. It's truly supernatural love.

Another modern-day example of this is Shawn Bolz. He operates in present day prophetic ministry. I don't personally know him but from the interactions I've seen him have with people in live conferences and on YouTube, he seems to be extremely down to earth, compassionate, and funny. He has countless testimonies you can watch from YouTube with complete strangers, demonstrating God's supernatural love in profound ways. There are tons of examples of him giving "words of knowledge" and prophetic words for people that have proven to be incredibly accurate. As I've seen first-hand, this isn't exclusive just to him or anybody. It's available for you and me too. I've been brought to tears so often seeing how specific God can speak into a person's life who was in desperate need of a breakthrough. It's one of the New Covenant demonstrations of prophecy in the context of radical love rather than the fear, doom and gloom of the Old Covenant.

I encourage you to ask God for direction in your own life regarding the many areas we've covered in this journey together. The religious spirit is very deceptive and manipulate using fear, and false religious securities to maintain its prisoners. But where the Spirit of the Lord is there is FREEDOM; and no, I'm not referring to an immoral freedom, but a freedom in which every cell and part of your body, mind, soul and spirit have found their full satisfaction in union with God.

I found that next to every authentic sermon, book, or YouTube video on the supernatural working of God, is some religious alternative video or source warning you of the deception in that video. Some people have even created entire ministries warning everyone of the deceptions in these other churches and ministries. With my background with such warnings from E.G.W., these can be very alarming and disturbing at first glance. What can also make us vulnerable to believing such religious warnings again, is that the supernatural working of the Holy Spirit isn't restricted to look the way we say He should. With religious backgrounds, we would prefer God to give us a written outline or blueprint formula that says, *"These are the only ways I will manifest My presence and power and nothing else."* Such a cookie-cutter formula would make our flesh so much more confident and in control like we had with our religious formulas before. *But the supernatural is the very opposite of religion as it always depends on what the Holy Spirit is doing and saying for that moment, case by case, person by person*. (Jesus would say in the New Testament, "I only say what I hear My Father say and only do what I see Him do...") Therefore, with the supernatural, our only confidence is in depending on the Holy Spirit for wisdom and discernment especially when we see someone manifesting in a way that offends what we have believed in our life. We also need to test everything by the scriptures, because God would never contradict His written Word by something supernatural. But He also isn't restricted to only heal in the various ways exemplified in scripture, (mud on someone's eyes, etc.), or manifest only in the examples He gave us in Scripture. The examples of supernatural encounters, miracles, signs and wonders all throughout the Bible are to raise our expectancy of God doing the impossible today, rather than being a ceiling or formula we restrict Him to. That is very important to keep in mind as we are led by the Holy Spirit into more supernatural realities of the kingdom. Remember, prior to Peter's experience of walking on water, Philips translocation, or Lazarus' resurrection, there was no Scripture for these guys to point back to. People had to either believe it was from God or Satan, based on what they believed the _nature of God_ was like according to Scripture.

Imagine the criticism they must have received from the religious church leaders who labeled such things as demonic, because they had no personal experiences like this in the church. I have found this to be no different today regarding the supernatural things God continues to do. He enjoys keeping us in awe and wonder of His works. But such spontaneity and unpredictability makes the flesh and religious mind crazy because there's no way of us humanly controlling that. But we are invited to a fuller surrender to God's leading and God's ways. "For those led by the Spirit of God are sons of God." Romans 8:14. The ways He chooses to manifest, deliver, heal, and reveal Himself to a person or congregation during a service, may look entirely different each time. However, the fruit that follows will show genuine, authentic, transformation if He was the one who truly touched them. That fruit is what is easiest to test according to scripture. He never said, "By the manifestation we'll know them," but "By their fruits you will know them."

Sometimes when the Holy Spirit is delivering somebody from a demon, they can shake, tremble, scream, vomit, salivate, etc. This can be alarming, but to then see the peace of God come over that same person right after, is absolutely incredible and a testament to the powerful Gospel in present day reality.

Everyone reacts differently to the presence and power of the Holy Spirit because everyone is so uniquely different and He's very personal just as Jesus is. I've seen some people encounter Him and start to hysterically laugh and act childlike similarly to people who have drank alcohol. I was really turned off by this and believed it had to be demonic. But then God began to test my quick religious analysis saying, *"If the manifestation is truly from Me, their life afterward will show the fruit. If it's not from Me, then their life will remain unchanged."* Sure enough, this has proven to be true. I later heard the testimony of such an individual who was acting childlike and drunk, and that they had been oppressed by depression for over a decade due to a traumatic loss of a child. This "Holy laughter" was God's way of delivering them not merely for a momentary emotional high, but as a sign that their sorrow was tuning into gladness and joy. That's exactly what followed afterward in the person's life as they were radically delivered and on fire for God.

When the manifestation was not genuine, demonic, or coming from a person's need for attention (their flesh), there would be nothing that followed afterward. But on the surface, both appeared exactly the same. Just as in scripture, there was always a counterfeit that appeared to look like the genuine (Moses versus the magicians, sorcerers versus Apostles). But God is not intimidated by the devil's ability to create a fake manifestation. If He was, He could just eliminate that from being a possibility. Instead, He knows, *"My sheep hear My voice and I know them and they know me...⁵ And a stranger will they not follow, but will flee from him: for they know not the voice of strangers. and they won't listen."* (Jn. 10:27, 5 KJV). The devil can never create the genuine change and transformation that the gospel can.

When we witness a manifestation of some sort that makes us uncomfortable, that is when we need the comforter (Holy Spirit) more than ever. He is there to help us see beyond our own offense and into the revelation beyond the surface appearance. That revelation could be God telling you, "Don't judge that ministry or that person by that particular video clip from a particular church service, because that manifestation may have been exactly what was needed for that congregation but it's not a full picture of what they believe." When I've found myself trying to label something as demonic based off a video clip of manifestations, sometimes God would tell me to read one of their books to get a fuller picture of what they believe about Him. I listened and, as I read, I would be floored at the incredible revelation, spiritual maturity, and character revealed throughout their book which I totally would have missed had I decided to label them based on an isolated snapshot from a video. (The religious critics often use such out of context clips to create fear and warning videos as a way of validating their own ministries)

I'd encourage you to entrust yourself to the Holy Spirit's leading to new resources, relationships, ministries, and sources that can fuel your spiritual growth in alignment with New Covenant realities. You can't continue to drink from stagnant waters or ministry resources that do not believe in nor demonstrate the New Covenant realities of scripture and expect to get New Covenant mindsets and fruit. I've mentioned several New Covenant resources throughout this book that have been such a blessing to me. But even still this is merely scratching the surface of all the places God is currently manifesting His power and presence.

I did not begin my journey with analyzing what is wrong with religion or Adventism. I began by wanting to experience more intimacy with Jesus. I want more of Him, His fruit, and His life to be in me. Like He did in the beginning, He invited me to learn more on what following Him looks like in my practical life, rather than merely reading and studying about Him. The more I grow in learning His voice and His ways, the more I want nothing more than to spend time in His presence. I've seen that the more my beliefs align with His heart, the more scripture *clearly* flows together without needing religious lenses to explain away an obvious truth. I become more engaged with His realm on an everyday basis. Passages or verses I would have glossed over or tried to humanly reason away now make sense as I not only understand them but I'm experiencing the reality of them in my life.

I pray, even now, you ask Holy Spirit to give you ears to hear and eyes to see His realities and invitations for you to personally experience in the New Covenant reality. There is no other person in heaven or earth more willing and qualified to reveal God to you than the Holy Spirit. His indwelling us, is what everything in the Old Covenant pointed forward to as our NOW inheritance gained through Jesus' blood of the New Covenant. The spiritual truths, realities and experiences that follow are clearly shown example after example in the book of Acts and in modern day testimonies all around wherever

He is truly present. Would you dare entrust your heart fully to His leading? Would you dare to give Him all of you? Make this fuller surrender something intimately personal just between you and Him. I promise it is the best, most exciting thing you could ever do.

Shattering
RELIGION'S
HOLLOW SHELL